SIMPLY
SIGNIFICANT

SIMPLY SIGNIFICANT

achieving a legacy beyond success

Anne K. Chinoda

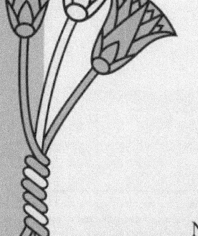

New York

Simply Significant
Achieving a Legacy Beyond Success

Cover design and interior graphics by Bill Sprau, www.Sprau.net
Author photograph by Michael Cairns, www.MichaelCairns.com

ISBN 978-1-60037-598-9

Library of Congress Control Number: 2009901213

MORGAN · JAMES
THE ENTREPRENEURIAL PUBLISHER

Morgan James Publishing, LLC
1225 Franklin Ave., STE 325
Garden City, NY 11530-1693
Toll Free 800-485-4943
www.MorganJamesPublishing.com

In an effort to support local communities, raise awareness and funds, Morgan James Publishing donates one percent of all book sales for the life of each book to Habitat for Humanity. Get involved today, visit **www.HelpHabitatForHumanity.org.**

This book is dedicated to the blood donors who give of themselves every day to save lives. They exemplify "significance" and their lives create a legacy for all to follow.

Contents

SIGNIFICANCE EXERCISES

Acknowledgments

We ourselves feel like we are nothing but a drop of water in the ocean, but I think that ocean would be less without that drop of water.

—Mother Teresa of Calcutta, missionary and humanitarian

Simply Significant is a dream come true for me, and I hope it can be an inspiration that helps you fulfill dreams in your life. There are many people I have to recognize in the completion of this work, as it could never have been done alone. This acknowledgment is one of the prime lessons of "significance." Only in finding our passions and in serving others with those gifts do we leave a legacy on this earth.

This book is the result of a twenty-five-year journey that culminated over the past five years with the development of a concept I hope will truly inspire you to seek and find significance. In addition, I want to change the paradigm of leadership for a new generation. That work requires the hands and hearts of many people.

I have to start with my husband, Alan, the love of my life. He has been there for every step and continues to stand beside me and encourage me in all that I do. My two sons, Mark and Alexander, are my inspiration and the two most important reasons I want to leave a legacy. I want to thank these three special men for their patience, love, and understanding. I also want to thank my mother and father for all they have contributed to my life. In the chapters that follow, I will take more time to share with you the deep perspective my father has shared and the important role he plays in this book.

Next I need to extend thanks to my immediate circle of collaborators, senior staff, board members, and colleagues. In conjunction with those individuals, I must also pay homage to the group of people who really inspired this book: the blood donors.

There is a team of people who have specifically collaborated with me on this book over the past five years. This team has been with me every step of the process and provided the essential work to help bring this from a dream to reality. Roy Reid, Bill Sprau, Wendy Kurtz, Pam MacKenzie, Diane Sears, Tim Vandehey, and Debbie Zmorenski worked tirelessly to bring out the essence of the book and provide greater clarity. Each of these very special people helped in the development of the concept, writing, and art for the book as well as additional content for corresponding presentations, workshops, and speeches. In addition, these individuals also stood beside me and provided me with inspiration and support when things got rough and it seemed the book might not be completed. For all of that, I am most grateful. Another key member of this team is my publisher, Morgan James Publishing, whose belief brought this work to market.

As important as my development team is the group of peers and CEOs who took time to read early drafts of the manuscript and provided essential input to sharpen the messages and real-life applications. This group of leaders includes Abboud Bejjani, Shannon Brouillette, Sally Caglioti, Ron Labrum, Daniel O'Day, David Perez, Merlyn Sayers, MD, Sandy Shugart, PhD, and Greg Sunset.

I am also blessed to have within my inner circle a team at Florida's Blood Centers that provides the strong leadership needed to deliver the right blood at the right time to the right person every day. The leadership and commitment to excellence these people share is the foundation on which we build our achievements at FBC. In addition, we are led by our fantastic board of directors, chaired by my mentor and colleague Leighton Yates. The board appointed me CEO in 2003 and has provided strong oversight and an extraordinary commitment to FBC's mission.

My acknowledgment of all these people is an important illustration of how we engage in life and its challenges as significant people. It is through the challenges we face in life and the ways we interact with people that we hone and sharpen our significance and ultimately create our legacy. Let me illustrate this point with a practical explanation I have used in a number of presentations:

The Smooth Stone

Let me engage your senses for a moment to illustrate significance. Consider a smooth black stone. If you take it and hold it for a moment, you can feel that the stone's smoothness is calming; it fits comfortably in your hand. Many people use stones like this to build a feng shui rock garden, or just hold them to relax or meditate. What's important to know about the stone is that it did not begin its life as a smooth stone. It began as a rock: jagged, big, and bulky. Over time, it was shaped through intense pressures, perhaps from pounding water, the harsh elements, or even artisans. This is a metaphor for our lives. The sculptor uses a hammer and chisel to pound a large stone into a beautiful work of art. Life's trials and tests shape us in the same way. People and difficult issues can be like those harsh elements that pound on us and may even feel like they will break us. However, we also have good experiences and encounter good people, both of which provide the encouragement and love that is like the polishing cloth which brings the stone to its perfect final condition. Be courageous in your most challenging moments—step forward and be significant for someone else every time challenges come your way. Over time, you will become a resource where others find comfort and fulfillment, which in turn strengthens you to face even greater challenges and achieve more than you can imagine.

We are all on a journey to significance. I pray that you are able to find it here and build a legacy of hope. As you discover your calling and build your legacy, I would be honored if you would share your observations, challenges, and accomplishments at my website, www.SimplySignificant.com.

Warmest wishes,
Anne

Foreword

Let me first say "Congratulations!" You may not realize it yet, but by picking up this book, you have made the first step on a path toward a fuller life, greater fulfillment, and more happiness and honor in all you do. Through unique and effective storytelling, self-evaluation, and guiding principles, this book compels people to be simply *significant.* The word "significant" might sound ambiguous to you now; however, after reading this book you will see there are simple but critical things you can do in your daily life to ensure your footing is firmly on the path to significance.

When Anne Chinoda first approached me with this book in its early stages of development, I was excited for her and honored she had asked me, as a colleague and friend, to critique her ideas. As I reflected on Anne's ambition to publish this book, on top of the countless roles and responsibilities she takes on—president and CEO, wife, mother, friend, author, daughter, board member, volunteer (the list goes on)—it reminded me of something a friend once said to me. I commented on how busy life can be, on a day when I had a particularly overwhelming number of things ahead of me to do, and he said, "*Well, there's never enough time to do everything, but there is always enough time to do the most important thing.*"

I'm sure he meant all I had to do was prioritize and take care of a few of the big items before tackling the rest of my to-dos. But, later, as I looked at Anne's manuscript, piled on my desk among many items that demanded my attention, I thought, "*This is important.*" Little did I know *how* important reading Anne's book would be for her ... and me!

I won't describe in detail how much I learned from Anne's ideas, but I will say that her book *touches you in a personal way, and by reading it, you will be touched.* As for content, well, you'll just have to keep reading and see for yourself. However, if you are open-minded and take time to internalize and reflect on Anne's messages, I can promise you will learn. Anne's book reinforced for me my personal philosophy for learning, which is to always ask, "What happened, what did I learn, and what will I do differently going forward?" The stories and messages in this book brought back many memories of lessons learned—and many memories of where I failed to learn at the time, but now have the opportunity to do things differently going forward.

Let me also add that Anne's book exemplifies the truth in the quote I just mentioned. We have only one life to live. The choices we make each day and what we do with the small moments we have are what reflect a life well-lived, and these determine significance versus mere success.

Take a moment to think of all the roles you play, all the hats you wear, all your competing priorities. I'm sure you know which ones *should* take priority. This book will help you find another layer in life. After priority comes *significance,* because there is a difference between *importance* and *impact.* Most things you do are important or you wouldn't waste your time on them. Anne's book will teach you how to fuse your time, your objectives, your beliefs and values, your enthusiasm, and even your bottom line so everything you do impacts and influences people and situations for the better. That is significance.

After reading this book, you will be reminded that the time you have is what you make of it, and it's the little things you do—like sending out a recognition note for a favor, pointing out a person's positive qualities, spotting a need and filling it, or finding time to help a friend— that truly are the measure of your significance. Actually, being significant isn't the tough part; it's simple to do great things for yourself and others once you see how good it feels. The tough part is making the choice to take the path to significance. That's why I started with "Congratulations!" You've made the choice, but it's up to you to stay on course. Luckily, Anne has given you an incredible roadmap to guide you on your way.

Best of luck,

David B. Perez
President and CEO
CaridianBCT

Introduction

I am not going to share anything in these pages that you don't already know at some level. Nothing in here is new; my perspective on the material may be new, and certainly the stories I will share with you are fresh and original. My hope is that the concepts, and the manner in which they are presented, will help you find the clarity to live a more fulfilling and significant life, establish a framework for building and maintaining healthy relationships, become a more effective leader, and leave a legacy that inspires others.

Thousands of books are published each year about success—how to achieve it, maintain it, survive it. However, as you will see, and as you have probably experienced in your own life, success is both fleeting and subjective. Pursuing society's common definition of success as your life objective will eventually become disappointing, frustrate you with its "starts and stops" and perhaps lead to a state of corruption in which you sell out your personal morals and ethics for short-term gain.

You see, we are all born with a deep longing to fill a void in our lives with something more than the subjective and fleeting rewards of achievement in business, industry, technology, or education. Every one of us craves a deeper kind of satisfaction—a higher calling that is not tied to the bidding or approval of others or fueled by the selfish desires of a culture of greed. The irony is this: While significance usually leads to success, success does not always lead to significance. Those who focus on becoming significant will often ultimately become successful due in large part to the fact that they have achieved a sense of self-satisfaction and peace that will not be disrupted by the tides of life that come at us all.

What's the Difference?

Of course, before we can move on, we must ask a critical question:

What is the difference between success and significance?

It's not enough to automatically file "success" on the shelf marked "material gain at the expense of all else" because, to be fair, there are as many concepts of success as there are individuals. Some people define success purely according to the amount of money they earn and the material possessions they own. This is the Gordon Gecko, "Greed is good" stereotype that is most common in our culture. But others define success as having no debt and a secure job, while others define it as earning a living doing what they love, and so on. The key is that most often, success is defined by what we do to keep a roof over our heads, feed our families, save for retirement, and occasionally enjoy a vacation or special purchase. For the purposes of this book, we're going to stick with the most common definition of "success": earning as much money and owning as many enviable material possessions as possible. I think that is what most people, were they polled, would answer when asked "What comes to mind when you hear the word *success*?" so that's what I'll use.

Significance is something else again, something more difficult to define, yet far more transcendent. You find stark differences between *success* and *significance*. While success is the act of "doing," of action seeking approval or personal gain, significance is the act of "being." It is action with intent to serve. A person who seeks significance is looking to transform not just what he or she *does*, but what he or she *is*. Significance means becoming a source of positive change in the world, someone who improves the lives of others and embodies a set of qualities I see as the highest in humanity: honor, compassion, love, selflessness, courage, and the desire for justice, fairness, and truth. To define it formally:

> **Significance**: *Knowing who you are and aligning your energy with your life's true calling (and the opportunities it brings) so you can reach beyond yourself and contribute to the world in ways that bring hope to others and establish a cherished legacy.*

You can see that pursuing a life defined by such qualities has little to do with your material success—though it doesn't preclude extraordinary financial and career achievement. However, people who surrender to the siren song of monetary success and professional acclaim without making a *deliberate effort* to also pursue significance rarely achieve it. Living a life that transforms the world for others does not happen by accident.

Significance is also about honor, principles, and values, and so it represents a paradigm shift in the way we conduct our lives in this country. We have become a "sanction culture," meaning that we govern our behavior not by learning what is right and then doing it but by creating oversight and laws that penalize us when we act wrongly. But any restriction can be circumvented, and in the pursuit of success at all costs, that's exactly what many CEOs, financiers, and corporate leaders have done. Enron, Bear Stearns and other corporate collapses were the result of a "values vacuum" and carried out by people who made success priceless while valuing significance not at all.

In this book, we are going to examine the paradigm shift that must take place if we are to avoid becoming another decadent, fallen Roman Empire: a shift to an emphasis on teaching values, honor, and significance to our leaders.

The Essence of Being

In the coming pages, you and I are going to explore what it means to choose significance over success. We're going to look at how to determine what path you have chosen so far in your life, and you're going to discover how to gauge that for yourself. Most importantly, you will spend time with some exceptional human beings who are on their own "significance quests," and as a result, find your own path to significance—in effect, to find the essence of your being.

Significance is each person's *essence of being*. It is that calling from deep within that we all must find in order to create a sense of balance in our lives, a balance that affords us the position to pursue other objectives with purpose and intent. We have all either felt the need to "give something back" or heard about wealthy, wildly successful people who transform their lives and become incredibly dedicated to a cause larger than themselves. People like Bill Gates, who left Microsoft to dedicate the rest of his life and his huge fortune to running his foundation and, to name one goal, eradicating AIDS in Africa. What passion drives human beings to achieve incredible professional success and then decide that's not enough? What compels them to give vast amounts of money and time to change the lives of people they will never meet? I believe it is this:

> *We draw closest to our true selves when we are serving a cause greater than ourselves.*

It feels wonderful to give to something selflessly, to help another person or other people. It buoys our spirits and lifts our souls in a way that defies our consumer, debt-driven culture. That's what I mean by significance. You don't have to run a multibillion-dollar foundation to achieve it, either. All you must do is listen to the voice inside yourself telling you, "This is your purpose. This is what gives you meaning." Once you do that, significance becomes inevitable.

> **Essence of being:** *That which you feel "called" to do or pursue and which brings the ultimate meaning, purpose, joy, and fulfillment to your life.*

The footnote to this idea is that while the pursuit of significance over success leads to success, the pursuit of success alone typically corrupts. I don't necessarily mean corruption in the sense of bribery or graft, though that does occur. No, I'm talking about the corruption of those principles and ideals that are part of your essence. These slowly erode the more you pursue success at the cost of everything else. The progression is like a slow-moving disease: First the person chases success because of ego and the desire to accumulate wealth, always making the bargain that, "I'll give back when I have enough." But "enough" never comes; greed breeds greed, and the quest for greater success consumes all the time the person could be thinking about helping others or transforming the world. Eventually the relentless chase for success ends up costing this individual the relationships and idealism that would lead to a significant life. That is corruption, and everyone loses: the person, his or her family, and society at large.

My Father

This book is intended to help you discover those hidden, whispering aspects of yourself that will guide you toward achieving balance and finding significance. It's not an easy journey; it's important to understand there is great darkness in life that we must endure. In Chapter Two, "Success Versus Significance," we will look at some of the contributors to this darkness. We must make the choice to not let the darkness define us.

When considering significance, and especially the formation of a legacy that lives beyond oneself, I think back to the ancient Egyptians. The Egyptian culture was infatuated with breaching the line between life and death and with eluding personal extinction. Ancient Egyptians were passionate about becoming part of something significant that existed beyond their individual lives. In other words, they wanted to leave a legacy. They, like many of us today, wanted to know the purpose of their time on earth and wished to fulfill whatever it was they were put here to do. In my own life, my understanding of significance is reflected in both my own experiences and those lessons I have learned from my father. In addition, as president and CEO of Florida's Blood Centers, I am constantly surrounded by people who remain devoted to the ideal of personal significance. I meet and talk to blood donors each day. It is through their eyes and in their stories that I am constantly reminded of the importance of tapping into the "essence of our being" each day.

"Hindsight is 20/20." That phrase never meant so much to me as on the day I looked into my father's beautiful eyes and saw a man who was wishing he had lived the first part of his life as he is now living his last phase. In his career, my dad reached the pinnacle of material and professional success. He was a top executive with a major corporation and he lectured as a college professor. But as he reviewed his life, he realized he had spent it simply reaping the monetary benefits of fulfilling the destiny of others. From the outside, it was great. He provided well for his family and many people respected him. He had status, possessions, and praise.

But as his career came to a close, he felt empty. He felt bitter. He felt he had been used by others. He realized how much more he could have enjoyed life and his family had he operated from a center of his own choosing. What could life have been like if he had chosen to say no to situations when he felt compromised? What if he had traveled less and been home more? What if he had invested in the lives of people instead of stocks and bonds? My father's experience has shown me that the most IMPORTANT question a person can ask is, "What if?" And what's most rewarding for me is to see what he has done with the last 20 years as he has dedicated his life to a charity he began and to helping others in so many ways. Looking up his old friends and family to solicit contributions to an organization that provides needy children with bicycles, asking "what if" and challenging others to give more and do more. Today, "Bikes for Kids" is one of New England's most successful charities and a testimony to a man who himself could not afford a bicycle as a child. In addition, he has taken his life experiences and used them to try and help others find their opportunities to become significant and make a difference. At 82, my father is dynamic, vivacious and inspiring to all those he meets. And most importantly he knows that it is never too late and the best is yet to come.

Is this meant to say that making money is a bad thing, or that success is automatically empty and shallow? No—not if you *choose* to move beyond the quest for success to pursue a life of significance. You can find fulfillment if you seek first to become significant before you worry about success, because success *within* significance is a life lived with no regrets, a life lived to your highest purpose, heeding the voice of passion that shouts within every one of us.

Confessions of an Ex-Skater

We live in a society that has a "have it all" mentality, but often we define "having it all" in a dangerously shallow way. If we can focus on such simple goals as having a nice car, a nice house and enough money to retire, why then do we not choose to "have it all" when it comes to living a significant life—making a difference for others? My professional life has been a twenty-five-year lesson in how people find their own sense of significance through the act of giving blood. I am always dumbstruck to learn that, even though donors experience their own personal challenges, the act of giving blood seems to wash away their personal hurts and frustration, replacing them with the knowledge that they have done good. These donors carry out a lifesaving act with little to no need for recognition; for them, the act of goodness is reward enough. Every day, I meet and learn from these people as they give of themselves, and I have taken that lifelong lesson as a foundation for this book.

Early in my life, I learned about the weight of making decisions that could lead to regrets. I spent the majority of my childhood training in competitive figure skating. Skating was the defining aspect of my childhood and shaped much of my perspective. From ages four to seventeen, I traveled the country, worked with trainers and lived my days and many nights on the ice. I did reap many benefits from this experience: discipline, hard work, the ability to push myself physically and mentally to achieve goals far beyond my expectations. For all of those gifts, I am grateful. However, skating also consumed so much of my young life that I began to resent the idea of it as I approached adulthood. While I enjoyed the act and elegance of skating, I had much less appreciation for the competitive aspects. Love and affection seemed to be conditional, based on my accomplishments. I enjoyed praise and approval when I was winning, but felt like a failure when I did not win.

Late in my skating career, I realized I would have to sell out my love of the sport to reach the next competitive level. I would have to leave behind skating as a passion and turn it into my business. This was the defining choice of my future, and I chose to quit competitive skating. Many people thought I would regret my decision, but I have no such regrets.

Skating taught me hard lessons about the human condition. I learned that if your entire life is judged solely on performance, you leave others in charge of defining who you are and whether or not you have succeeded. You are always reaching upward but not inward. You miss out on life lessons. Instead of finding ways to work with others in your circle of influence and contribute to the wider world, you become isolated, looking only to your next professional milestone. This obsession leaves nothing but a hole in your soul. That is the difference between success and significance. As the saying goes, no one ever said on his or her deathbed, "I wish I had spent more time at work."

I am hardly perfect. I made what I know was the right decision to turn away from skating before it made me into the kind of person I did not want to become. But I still struggle every day with my own journey toward significance, and some days it is a real struggle that leaves me feeling as though I've been wrestling with angels: juggling the demands of my position as CEO, my charity and community work, this book, my family, and more. Some days I lose the battle. Other days, it's a tie. Still others, I'm too exhausted to care. But in the end, I think my personal scale tips on the side of bringing more light and hope to other human beings, which is what significance is about. At least, I hope it does. The battle never really is won.

Drops in the Ocean

Thanks to my career, I have the good fortune of talking to employees, volunteers, and donors who understand the empowerment and the possibilities that come with serving others. Too often, people in our materially obsessed culture begin to feel as if they are isolated, separated, and invisible. When this happens, we look outside of ourselves for validation, yearning for a sense of belonging. Mother Teresa understood this basic human need to matter, to try to alleviate the isolation we sometimes feel, when she said, "We ourselves feel that what we are doing is just a drop in an ocean. But the ocean would be less because of that missing drop."

This is what we all must understand about who we are and what we do. All of us contribute to the "ocean" in our own unique way. Without our contributions, the ocean would be missing something important. Once we come to this realization, it becomes vital that we change the orientation of our lives so that significance acquires a position of at least equal importance alongside success. We also must not underestimate our ability to accomplish significant things; significance is not only attained with awe-inspiring acts of greatness, but through small, ordinary acts of humanity and compassion. In fact, I would argue that small, anonymous acts of good are the greatest source of significance—of that elation and meaning we feel when we transform the world around us for the better—that will ever exist. Significance is about how our actions improve the lives of the people we influence and touch through our everyday interaction.

This book takes a deliberate but carefully chosen path through the idea of significance to bring you to knowledge and enlightenment. You will find:

- A look at both the dark and the light sides of life, intended to bring you to the crossroads of your choice: success or significance?
- A merciless light shone on the practices of today's leaders and an understanding of why the priorities we are teaching our CEOs, politicians, and other leaders must be transformed if we are to have a just, compassionate society that survives its challenges.
- A penetrating self-examination that will help you determine your "Significance Quotient," or SQ. How significant is your life today, and how much have you sacrificed true happiness for the pursuit of shallow successes?
- Several tools to help you on your journey. You are reading this book because you want to find that place in life where you can make a difference. You are also striving to be the best possible leader, whether in the home or at the helm of a major company. In Chapters Six through Ten, "keys" will help you find your way and uncover the attributes that lead to significance in any situation.

This is a profoundly emotional topic for me. I love what I do and I cherish the many ways in which my life reaches out to touch the lives of others. It's that contact that gives me purpose and meaning. Sometimes, the knowledge that my actions have the power to revive a spirit or change the course of a life is so humbling, it leaves me in tears. But if I allow emotion to rule the day for me, this book will be about my story, and it's not. It's about you. It's about you coming to understand the paradigm shift that significance represents and about redefining your own life course so you may find something more satisfying and elemental: the person you were meant to be.

Will you look back on today twenty years from now and be filled with regret for time lost or a life lived in judgment by others? Or will you take a stand and "choose significance"? It is now your time to choose. I'm honored to have the opportunity to help you make the choice that is wisest for your future.

PART ONE:
DO YOU REALLY WANT SUCCESS?

CHAPTER ONE
Choosing Significance: A Parable

A FICTIONAL CHARACTER'S JOURNEY TO DISCOVER HIS "ESSENCE OF BEING" AND LIVE A SIGNIFICANT LIFE

> *The significance of a man is not in what he attains, but rather what he longs to attain.*
>
> *—Kahlil Gibran, poet*

Jim walked out of his morning meeting feeling great. A prospective client, a small, family-owned bakery, had secured the funds to open a new location in town and approached Jim's firm to design it. This wasn't a big account, but Jim was moved by the owner's enthusiasm and determination. Plus, Jim knew what it was like to start from the ground up, and he was happy for the opportunity to help a mom-and-pop business that probably was up against a lot of competition in the marketplace from corporate-owned chains.

As he rounded the corner to his office, his secretary, Susan, bolted up from her seat. "Boy, are you in demand today," she said, handing him a stack of messages, mail, and other documents. "You sure look calm for someone whose phone has been ringing off the hook and has a million incoming e-mails." In the meeting, Jim's Blackberry, which left his side only when he was in the shower or in bed, had buzzed repeatedly, serving as a reminder of the busy day ahead of him.

But he hadn't had a chance to review the messages and calls that had been coming in; he'd been busy with this new client. All in a day's work.

"I wouldn't be able to keep up with it all if you didn't keep me in line," he told Susan sincerely. Susan's tenure as his secretary was going on ten years, and Jim wasn't sure how he'd ever managed without her. He often wondered if she ever grew tired of her job, but she continued to come in every day with a positive attitude and energy that he greatly admired and appreciated. She certainly made his life easier, and clients were constantly commenting to him on her personable, professional nature.

"Randy has been calling all morning," she told him. "He tried your cell, but I told him you were in a meeting." She looked concerned. "You should get back to him. He didn't sound like himself."

Jim sighed. Randy again. Jim's nephew, who was in his late thirties, was a rising star at a fairly large law firm. The two had always been close. While they weren't in the same field, Jim had always served as an unofficial mentor to Randy as he was growing up, giving him guidance when it came to sports, friends, girls, college, and now, life in the workforce. They usually spoke on a weekly basis, but lately, he'd been hearing less and less from the young attorney. Randy was working hard, trying to secure a position as partner.

Jim worried about the kid. He was rising quickly through the ranks, but Jim was familiar with the costs of trying to climb the corporate ladder. The symptoms of the tiring pursuit of success were showing. Randy often sounded exhausted on the phone; his mood depended on the day and the status of whatever case he was working on. He had also missed quite a few family functions, and at the last one where he'd made an appearance, Jim remembered there had been a fight between Randy and his teenage daughter, Tess, over Randy's being unavailable to help her prepare for her driving test, weekend after weekend, because of work. The argument had ended with Tess in tears and grounded for lashing out at her father. To Jim, it was a warning sign that the imbalance in his nephew's life was reaching the critical point.

"Well, it's almost eleven o'clock," Jim said to Susan. "Do me a favor and tell Randy I'm stopping by. See if he can join me for lunch." Knowing very well his nephew would resist with the usual response of "too much work," Jim also knew Randy needed a break. Plus, he had other plans in store for that afternoon.

Tapping a Vein of Personal Satisfaction

As he left his office on the way out of the building, a unique beep from his Blackberry reminded Jim it was almost time for his regular appointment ... an appointment with significance. He didn't think of it that way, of course. To him, this regular commitment was something that bestowed upon him a deep and glowing satisfaction. He walked past the plaques on the wall that heralded his achievements and honors. No big deal. He didn't tell anyone where he was going for this appointment; he never did. It was private and personal. Even Susan, his gatekeeper, wasn't sure where he went every other month. But today he was going to take Randy along for the experience.

Street sounds of car horns, construction, and shouts for taxis surrounded him as he made his way down the few blocks between his office and Randy's law firm. People became a blur in the quick-paced flow of traffic on the sidewalk. Almost everyone seemed frustrated, stressed, harried. Tires squealed and tempers flared as a frantic pedestrian with an iPhone glued to his ear tried to beat the DON'T WALK sign. But to an outside observer, Jim appeared immune to the cacophony around him. His face instead showed a feeling of deep satisfaction. He was looking forward to sharing an experience with Randy that he hoped would help the younger man find some contentment and purpose, even if life lately seemed overwhelming with work and worry. Jim knew he had a chance to save two lives that day.

He didn't do it for the accolades. He didn't do it so his board members would notice. He did it because it was a good thing to do and was part of his personal mission. Jim contributed when it was not required and would not directly benefit from what others thought of as his "success." He hoped Randy, too, would see the satisfaction that comes from making the choice to honor one's significance and put living by personal values and beliefs at the top of life's priority list—ahead of financial gain and career advancement. Jim was a blood donor.

Being Used

As Randy's paralegal led Jim to his nephew's office, he could see Randy was busy on the phone, pacing back and forth, his brow furrowed. Completely absorbed in the conversation, he took a moment to notice that his uncle had entered his office. Not wanting to interrupt, Jim sat patiently listening to Randy, who was obviously on the line with a client … or perhaps a more senior partner, given his particularly professional tone and consenting manner.

When the conversation ended a few minutes later, Randy slammed the phone down and plopped into his seat, bringing out a bit of the kid Jim always knew. His voice instantly became more animated, more exasperated. "What a week!" he groaned before Jim even had a chance to ask. "I've been on that call, but I got a note from Susan about lunch. I just can't today. There's a lunch meeting. And on top of all this casework, I'm trying to manage a community event for the firm, then there's this committee meeting at five o'clock tonight. And if I miss dinner one more time …" He trailed off mid-rant as if he'd become lost staring at the piles of paper strewn across his desk, or frozen in horror at the thought of what his wife might do if he didn't make it home in time for a family meal.

"I've really needed to talk to you lately, but honestly I'll be lucky if I can chat for a few minutes before I'm pulled into that lunch meeting," he finally said.

"Well, first, it's nice to see you, too," Jim said, teasing the young man for his frantic greeting. "And I knew you'd say that. But you've got almost an hour before lunch, so I thought we might take a walk, catch up for a bit. You could get some things off your chest. Plus, I've got something I want you to see."

The anxiety-ridden Randy took a bit more convincing, but soon the two men set off down the street, their destination unknown to the young attorney, who launched into a tirade about his trials and tribulations. Jim listened intently, conscious that Randy's stories were all too familiar. Yes, he could relate to the stress and dissatisfaction, since he, as a younger professional, had been obsessively, compulsively wrapped up in the constant quest for status and financial success. He saw himself in Randy and was determined that the younger man would not make the same mistakes he did.

As they walked, Randy constantly fidgeted with his phone, inspecting the calls and text messages coming in. Most of them, he explained, were about the firm's annual fundraising golf tournament, an event he took charge of this year in order to shine for the senior partners. But the whole thing was a chaotic mess, and sorting out and fixing the problems with contracts, celebrity appearances and sponsorships was a nightmare. On top of that, Sal, one of his firm's most valuable clients, roped Randy into serving as president of the Yacht Club, and Randy didn't even have time for the meetings, let alone time to fulfill the duties of club president or even enjoy his own boat.

But the main source of Randy's frustration and stress, Jim saw, was Eric, a bright young junior associate. Randy had been mentoring and guiding the young man since he was fresh out of law school. But for the past few months he'd also been helping with—or, more accurately, *doing*—most of Eric's casework. Randy had never mentioned this to anyone for fear that his decision to recruit someone who couldn't pull his weight would jeopardize Randy's standing in the firm. But the worst of it had come the previous week. The partners had called Randy in for his annual review and told him they were *promoting Eric to senior associate* because of his exemplary work—work Randy had largely done—while passing Randy up for promotion to partner. He'd been doing so much of Eric's work that his own work and demeanor had suffered, and this was the result.

Jim conveyed his sympathy, but he didn't find what had happened to Randy all that hard to believe. He knew it was easy to get so concerned with status, appearance, and the expectations of others that you could forget about your own needs and personal passions. Randy was being consumed, stretching himself too thin in his pursuit of success. Jim's heart went out to Randy as he listened to his nephew's worries about his mortgage, his mounting credit card debt and his fear that he was falling short in his family life. On the outside, Randy was an extremely successful young attorney, a shooting star. He was in the right social circles and his kids were in the right schools. But Randy didn't yet realize all that matters in life is what's inside. He was in danger of falling into that endless cycle of struggle, self-doubt, and further struggle that could only end in personal, relationship, or health breakdown—a state the Japanese call *karoshi*, literally "death from overwork."

Almost on cue, the two arrived at their destination.

Significance Exercise #1: Are You Being Used?

Being used by others is one of the fundamental signs of a life not oriented in significance. Being used doesn't mean you're being manipulated; rather, it means you're wandering purposelessly in your life and career while most of your time, effort, energy, and passion go to fulfill the goals of someone else. Is that the state you're in?

Select the appropriate answer as it applies to your professional or personal life. Give yourself one point for each a), two points for each b), and three points for each c).

Professional	Answers
1. I feel like I spend most of my career on a treadmill.	a) Frequently b) Occasionally c) Never
2. I allow others to take credit for the work I have done.	a) Frequently b) Occasionally c) Never
3. In my profession, I spend most of my time focused on surviving rather than thriving.	a) Frequently b) Occasionally c) Never
4. I fantasize about the career I could have had if I had followed my heart instead of playing it safe.	a) Frequently b) Occasionally c) Never
5. I feel like others earn the rewards and status for my excellence and dedication.	a) Frequently b) Occasionally c) Never
6. I feel stuck in a game in which I have no control over the rules.	a) Frequently b) Occasionally c) Never
Personal	
7. I don't tell my loved ones about my aspirations; they wouldn't understand.	a) Frequently b) Occasionally c) Never
8. I feel trapped by my obligations.	a) Frequently b) Occasionally c) Never
9. I feel enslaved to material possessions and the debt I've incurred to acquire them.	a) Frequently b) Occasionally c) Never
10. I want to give back to the community but never feel I have the time.	a) Frequently b) Occasionally c) Never
11. I feel like some of the people in my life have surpassed me, and it embarrasses me.	a) Frequently b) Occasionally c) Never
12. I dream sometimes about chucking everything and starting over on my own.	a) Frequently b) Occasionally c) Never

Scoring

30-36 points: You're in great shape. You are not being used by anyone, and you are probably very happy in your life and career and well on your way to significance.

21-29 points: You're being used in some area of your life and it's affecting your happiness and personal development. Your mission, should you decide to accept it: Find out how you're being used and by whom.

12-20 points: You're being used in multiple areas of your professional and personal lives, probably living mostly to please others. That is the cause of the frustration and lack of inspiration you almost certainly feel. You need to reassess everything about your course and begin making changes NOW.

Doing Nothing but Doing Everything

"Here it is," Jim said, smiling.

Randy looked startled as they stopped in front of the steps of the downtown blood bank. "This is what you wanted to show me? What? Did your firm do some work here?"

Jim laughed. "Nope, but, I think you'll like this place. It seems like work's taking too much out of you. They take from you here, too, but I think you'll find you get a lot more out of the little bit you give."

As they reached the blood center doors, Randy stepped into the path of a woman whose arms were stacked with papers before she could reach the door. As he scurried to open the door for her, she gave him an appreciative nod and broke into a smile as she saw Jim. She recognized him from his frequent visits.

"Hey there, stranger," she said. "And thank *you* very much," she said to Randy, entering into the center. "I am a little overloaded today."

"No problem, glad to help," Randy said as they all approached the registration desk.

"Are you here to donate today, too?" she tilted her head at Randy.

"Well, I guess I am now," Randy said, smirking at his uncle. "I didn't know we were coming here today, but I guess there's a first for everything. ... I've never given blood before. What about you?"

"I'm a regular donor," the woman said. "But today I'm here as a volunteer. I am a corporate trainer by profession and lend a hand on occasion to train new volunteers for the blood center. I work it in once a month as new volunteers come on board. I really don't have time to do it, but it means a lot to me."

"What got you started?" Randy asked.

"Well, when I was a first-timer like you, I was terrified. I was only doing it because my brother was facing major surgery. A sweet little lady who was volunteering that day saw how frightened I was. She stayed with me the whole time. As I finished, she thanked me and said she hoped I would come back because there are many people in need who do not have a sister to give for them. There was something in her eyes that captivated me.

"My brother made it through his surgery fine. For some reason, that experience lit a fire inside of me that made giving blood and helping here a part of who I am. The time I spend helping here seems to always be redeemed somehow. Ask your friend over there," she said, nodding at Jim. "He's in here all the time. I'll bet he feels the same way."

Jim smiled. "I do what I can."

Randy smiled, too, for what Jim imagined was the first time in a while. Jim thought, *Maybe this really will work.*

After they were led to their donor chairs, Randy looked over at Jim with a sly smile and said, "I guess you're lucky I'm not scared of needles, huh?"

Jim grinned. "I've been doing this for so long, I didn't even think to ask. Thanks for being a sport."

"No problem," Randy said. "I never realized you were a regular donor. I guess I just figured you wouldn't have the time to do something like this, but now I see it's a lot more quick and simple than I'd assumed. There's a food bank right down the street from the firm, and a buddy of mine is always asking me to volunteer there. But I just figured I was too busy to make any sort of commitment that would actually make a difference."

Randy looked around at the other people who were donating blood, people of all ages, races, and economic levels. The only consistent thing was that the life flowing out of their arms into their donor bags was the same color: red. "I guess I was wrong," he said, more to himself than to Jim.

Inwardly, Jim high-fived himself. This was the effect he'd hoped the visit would have. Randy had at least seen how simple doing something significant could be—really, it involved doing nothing but making the decision to take time to come in and sit for a few minutes. He hoped this glimpse of what was possible would help Randy look up from the self-imposed burden of his life and see, as Jim did many years ago, that committing to significance isn't a matter of time … it's a way of life. It's a choice.

The Art of Mentoring, Modernized
(From the Boston Globe)

Organizations have started to see the value of mentoring for enhancing work life, performance, commitment, and job satisfaction, and are creating new mentoring strategies to take advantage of these benefits. Mentoring has made the transition from one-on-one interaction to group practice and now often involves a peer-to-peer rather than junior-to-senior relationship. "There are still examples of traditional mentoring, but they are much rarer because of the nature of careers and organizations," says Boston University professor Kathy Kram. "The pace of change is much greater. It's unlikely that one mentor can meet all your needs." Mentoring "circles" engage in open-ended meetings that have space not just for networking and mutual learning, but also reflection on numerous subjects; such circles offer an opportunity to "think about larger-picture issues, like how to make the profession better," notes Boston attorney Deborah DosSantos. Mentoring plays an important role in American Express Co.'s initiatives to retain institutional knowledge by having exiting employees enrolled in a new phased retirement program mentor their successors.

The Storyteller

Jim stared at his blood dripping through the tubing and visualized a father, mother, son, or daughter who might benefit from his donation. He knew he might not be solving the problems of the world, but that he would help someone have the chance to smile again. Seeing the thoughtful grin on Randy's face, Jim knew one of those people was sitting right next to him.

He thought back to his knowledge of world religions. Blood is sacred in many faiths as a symbol of atonement or power. The people in the blood center that day were united spiritually with each other and donors in other centers around the country. By seeking lives of spiritual significance, these donors were literally saving lives.

As Jim and Randy left the blood center, Randy pointed out a plaque recognizing philanthropic volunteers and donors who helped the agency fulfill its mission. Many of the people listed had died years before. "It's great that the center still recognizes these people," he commented. "I bet they would be proud to know we noticed their names on the wall so many years later. Sometimes at work, I wonder if anyone will remember the things I've done … or if that stuff is even worth remembering."

Jim peered at his nephew, hearing an introspective tone he hadn't heard from the young lawyer in years. Randy's keen mind was lost in thought, and Jim thought surely the experience of giving blood was going to have an impact on him. It would be only one step of many, but it would be the first step. He hoped Randy would direct his intelligence, passion, and energy toward the things that made him truly happy, things that made a difference and would allow him to leave his own legacy.

"Speaking of work, I really do need to get back," Randy said, bringing Jim out of his thoughts. "I might just take a few things with me to finish up at home and ask someone to take notes for me at that committee meeting tonight. I feel like I haven't seen the kids in forever." He paused. "Thanks again, Jim. Let's do this again. Maybe you can even come to that shelter I was talking about sometime."

"Absolutely," Jim said. As Randy walked away with a wave, he couldn't help breaking out into a huge grin. Then he realized his stomach was rumbling, so he stopped in the family-run deli around the corner from his building. He placed his order, then heard a giggle that pealed throughout the old building:

"Grandpa, that's silly!"

At the other end of the counter was a little boy about five years old, ready to take a bite out of one of the deli's famous foot-long hotdogs. Sitting next to him was his grandfather, a dignified man with nimble hands and a broad grin. He had missed what the grandfather had done that was silly, but he noticed the boy and the old man shared the same twinkling, liquid brown eyes. He was reminded of himself and Randy, teacher and student.

The grandfather spoke so softly that Jim couldn't hear, but he was moving his hands in large gestures, apparently weaving a tale of intrigue. The boy was so glued to the old man's words, he forgot about the hot dog. Then he said, "No way!"

"It's all true, I swear," Grandpa rumbled in a silky, deep voice.

"Cute kid, huh?" Jim's waitress said as she brought his sandwich.

"Sure is."

"They come in here every Tuesday at noon. I find myself checking the clock to see if it's time for them to come in yet."

Jim looked up at his server and noticed she wasn't as young as he'd thought. He'd seen her here before but had never noticed her tired eyes, which he imagined came from early mornings and hours on her feet at the diner. "I'm sure they look forward to seeing you, too," Jim said, thinking that with a job like hers, she might not hear much positive feedback. But what she said next took him by surprise.

"Oh, I have no doubt they do," she said, smiling widely as she looked over at the little boy and he gave her a big grin. "That child has been coming in here since he was too tiny to walk or talk, and I've watched him grow up over the years. Once he told me I was his diner-grandma," she said with a laugh. "That's one of the reasons I love my job," she continued. "You get to meet so many different kinds of people in here. It's almost like I've been able to create a whole other family."

"That's a great way to look at it," Jim said, realizing that personal connections were part of the reason he, too, enjoyed his job. As his business had grown, he'd enjoyed establishing relationships with employees, clients, and vendors—finding out about their families, their favorite pastimes, and their passions. It made his work all the more rewarding.

"Well, I'll let you get back to your lunch now," the waitress said with a wink. She knew Jim was a regular, too. Jim turned his attention back to the end of the counter as the grandfather continued telling a tale that involved flinging an invisible fishing line and reeling in a big fish. The tale ended and the boy giggled, "That's my favorite." The grandfather paid the bill and the two walked toward the door, passing Jim.

"That's a nice-looking young man you've got there," Jim remarked to the elderly man.

"He's my grandpa!" the boy exclaimed proudly. Grandpa beamed and extended his hand, introducing himself and Hunter, his grandson.

"This is our weekly date," he said. "Some kids go to the library for story time. We just come here and I get to reminisce. For some reason, he never tires of the same old stories I tell."

Jim thanked them, and the two left, with the grandfather grinning and Hunter skipping. Jim thought as he paid his bill and headed back to the office how lucky the boy was. He would carry the memory of those stories, told again and again, for all his life and pass them on to his children someday. That, and the time his grandfather gave to him every week, would be Grandpa's legacy. A lucky boy, indeed.

Significance Exercise #2: Storytelling

We all have stories in our lives. Sometimes they are the myths of our family and the tales we wrap around ourselves to motivate us to become what we imagine. Other times, they are simply family history that we share. What stories are central to your life, and how have they affected you?

Describe the three stories that have been most important in your life so far. They could be family history, visions of what your future will be like, or even fictional tales that inspired you.

Story #1:

What this story means to you:	Do you share it with others? Why or why not?

Story #2:

What this story means to you:	Do you share it with others? Why or why not?

Story #3:

What this story means to you:	Do you share it with others? Why or why not?

The Journey

Back at the office, Jim removed the bandage and gauze applied at the blood center from his arm and thought back. When did it click for him, as it had not yet for Randy, that success was never going to be enough? When did he open his heart to significance? He knew. It was the first day he realized how empty success can be by itself. It was the day, years ago, when his father had stepped in and opened his eyes to everything his life was missing.

Jim had reached his pinnacle of professional success. Much like Randy, he was living a life of luxury. He had a beautiful house, a vacation home, and the money to buy two beautiful dream cars and a boat, and his family vacationed in elegant resorts. He had a lovely and caring wife and two children who were thriving. The picture was perfect, but Jim was depressed. He had worked hard to reach the top. He'd put in long hours to climb the ranks and had become the youngest president in his company's history. He held leadership roles in professional organizations, and he knew all of the bigwigs in the business. His projects had won awards and his annual salary had amounted to more than he'd ever imagined. But something was missing … something meaningful. Jim became frustrated that his success could be taken no further and his past achievements seemed so easily forgotten. He thought of what Plutarch wrote of the young Alexander the Great: "When Alexander saw the breadth of his domain he wept, for there were no more worlds to conquer. …"

One year, at an annual party held by Jim's company, his employees and shareholders had decided to give him their "Lifetime Achievement" award. Jim was one of only three people in the organization's history to have earned the award, but upon accepting it, he felt emptier than ever. After accepting hugs and handshakes, he sat down at an empty table, wanting to be alone with his thoughts. Then, after a few minutes, Jim's father approached him with a small box in hand.

"I'm very proud of you, son," he said, though his solemn look made the occasion seem more serious than celebratory. "I've been waiting to give this to you for a while now. I just hope you understand it." With that, his father walked away, leaving Jim to unwrap the small package. Inside the box was a brief note that read:

> *Through the years, I've watched you grow and learn. I've watched you find your voice and reach success after success. But lately I've watched you search. I know your success has left you feeling empty and feeling there must be something more. I think after all this time you are still trying to find yourself. I've used the enclosed words*

*as the guiding light for my life, and I hope they will help you open your eyes to all
you have to give.*

Curious, Jim unwrapped the gift and found a small plaque that was similar to the others in
his office. But the inscription was like nothing he had ever read before:

SIGNIFICANCE

*The state of knowing who you truly are—of aligning your energies
with your life's highest purpose in order to reach beyond yourself,
make a difference in the world, and leave a meaningful legacy.
After all, it is in serving others that we find ourselves.*

It was weeks before Jim understood the meaning behind his father's gift. Finally, frustrated
by his failure to grasp its meaning, it came to him: He needed to change the meaning of his
own success. His father was telling him that the next plateau lay in redefining who he was and
what he could do with the status he had achieved. He was called to begin making a difference
in his world. Just at the time when Jim began to realize the trek to success was never-ending,
he began plotting a path toward significance.

That path begins with unconditional love and ends with self-fulfillment and the
accomplishment of hopes and dreams. It is a journey on which the emphasis is placed on
others and not oneself. It is a journey anyone can take, regardless of income or station in life.
Jim took it and continues to take it. Days like this day, when he guided Randy subtly in the
direction of seeing something beyond his work, and took time to connect with the people in
the deli and realize they were on their own journeys, only reinforced his belief that he had
discovered something precious and rare.

Since that day, Jim's friends, family, and co-workers knew there was something stronger
about him and the way he lived life, made decisions, succeeded, and even failed. In all of his
endeavors he was guided by a drive to be significant. His journey was, and is, built on ideas
bigger than himself, yet it centers on the one thing that can fill his heart, mind, and soul with
contentment, something that's unique to him.

You have the same strength of purpose and powerful inner voice within you. This journey
will reveal it.

Next Steps for Significance Seekers ...

- *... Write down what you intend to do on a given day.*

- *... Keep a day journal and compare your intentions with what you really got done.*

- *... Step out of your normal routine and examine how you feel at the end of your typical day.*

- *... Make a list of people you know who seem especially joy-filled, purposeful, and mindful.*

- *... Ask yourself why those people have those qualities. What makes them different from you?*

CHAPTER TWO
Success Versus Significance

THE MEANING OF SUCCESS AND ITS HIDDEN PITFALLS, VERSUS THE SUBTLER NATURE OF SIGNIFICANCE, THE "ESSENCE OF BEING" THAT ALL OF US ARE SEEKING

It seems essential, in relationships and all tasks, that we concentrate only on what is most significant and important.
—Soren Kierkegaard, Danish philosopher and theologian

What is success? Society defines it as the achievement of goals or objectives based upon the measurement of society or a group of peers. Success brings fame, fortune, or notoriety. Just as telling, if a person chooses to give up the pursuit of professional status and financial reward in favor of raising children or pursuing a musician's life, most people would characterize him or her as "giving up on success." The fact is, if you chase success as it is most commonly defined, life is usually unfulfilling, leaving you exhausted and discontent. The lifelong pursuit of success often leaves its acolytes feeling so empty that they must begin feeding off other people, or turning to less virtuous means of finding satisfaction such as drugs, alcohol, or rampant spending.

Perhaps you're thinking, "This lady's crazy! Is she really saying success is a bad thing?" No. That would be both false and naïve. I don't think for a moment that man can live on aspirations and values alone, nor should you want to; it can be a joy to build a business, grow a career, and enjoy material comforts. I merely hope to show you there is more to life, that success is rarely ever sufficient for happiness *on its own*. The story you read in the opening chapter was meant to show you there are two tracks in life—*success* and *significance*—that often overlap, depending on your own experiences, interaction with others and station in life. Which one dominates in your own life is largely a matter of the choices you make—how you choose what matters most to you.

In his book *Lifeonomics: Living Free of Worry and Regret*, wealth manager and life coach Rob Holdford defines retirement as "The moment when you're certain that you will be able to spend the rest of your life doing what is truly important to you with the people who are truly important to you." That is how I would define significance: You know what is important to you in the core of your being—what you were put here on earth to do, what brings you happiness, fulfillment, satisfaction, and meaning—and you set out to reach the point where you can spend most of your time doing it. People who seek and achieve significance in their lives have a strong sense of what is genuinely important to their inner selves, and they can balance that with material and professional success.

> ***Success:*** *The achievement of a certain level of financial, material, and/or professional status that provides superficial security but acts as a drain on time, happiness, and connection with other people and the wider world.*

Significance Underneath

Success and significance go hand in hand, but they are not equal. Significance usually leads to success, but the equation rarely holds up in reverse. How does this work? In the story from the last chapter, Jim has achieved significance by becoming a blood donor and by paying attention to the personal relationships that enrich his life. He was already successful in his business, but when he discovered his significance, he became an *inspiration* to others. The people who worked with him admired his values and were more willing to follow his lead. Simply put, significance makes other people feel good about you, and that contributes to your success. Why did people travel halfway around the world to touch Mother Teresa? Why do thousands line up just to gain a glimpse of the Dalai Lama? Neither person represents great wealth or temporal power, but something in each stirs us at our deepest level. We feel the force of their purpose, their significance. When you have significance at your core, you have the ability to change people's hearts.

Success, however, does not guarantee significance. As we saw in Jim's story, pursuing success alone leaves us feeling unfulfilled and empty. Randy was by all accounts a successful lawyer, but he was miserable. He inspired no one because he had no purpose beyond advancing in his firm and making more money. There is nothing wrong with those goals, but they should not be your only goals. *The purpose of success is to serve your significance.* If not, then it is hollow and will eat away at your peace of mind and your security, because one hallmark of the single-minded pursuit of success is that it's never enough.

A Question of Balance

Life demands balance between the way we pursue our material and professional goals and the time and energy we devote to our passions. The more out-of-the-mainstream the passion—a wealthy stockbroker with a drive to be a blues musician, for example—the more determined we must be to make time and find the fire to pursue it. But there are two types of balance:

- **Other-Directed Balance**: The need to multitask and juggle numerous responsibilities that are geared toward pleasing others, with little time left for personal pursuits. These include taking on additional work to please a superior, getting involved in causes that advance one's social standing, and acquiring and maintaining new possessions in order to impress friends. Such people typically take on creative or charitable work not because of a burning desire, but because they feel obligated. But they rarely balance their work and status obsession with things that speak to their inner needs: vacations, hobbies, or personal passions.
- **Self-Directed Balance**: The ability to manage both professional and financial goals while giving sufficient time to pursuits intended to satisfy only the soul of the individual. These significant tasks might include personal, professional, and civic projects and regular duties that require time, energy, creativity, and emotional resources. Significance-balancers are able to say "yes" to tasks where the motive is to accomplish a purpose that is aligned to their core beliefs and life mission while still making a living. Such balance leaves a person feeling energized, enthusiastic, and excited about the journey of life.

What happens when your balance is all tilted toward pleasing others? Look at it this way: Success is a dangerous, powerful drug. Like any other drug, people can become addicted to it. They pursue success to define their lives. They use success as a measurement of how meaningful they are. But success is defined by society, not by us. The larger culture tells us we must have this car and that house and the other five-thousand-dollar watch. Why do some of us spend all our waking hours chasing trophies we neither want nor need? *Because striving for financial and professional success is easy.*

Think about it. Going after the corner office or the stock-option package requires no introspection. It demands no core beliefs. All it asks is that you devote all your time and energy to your goal. The trouble is, success doesn't inform you it's going to be moving the goalposts. Once you reach one plateau of success, you're expected to start climbing toward another. Once you become VP, you're compelled to go for CFO. Get there and nothing less than CEO will do, balance be damned. You're working 24/7/365. Never mind that by the time you reach that pinnacle, you're fifty-five years old, your children won't speak to you, and you hate everything about your job. If you don't keep compulsively climbing, you're a slacker, a loser.

I learned about this "trap of success" as a competitive ice skater. For every medal I won, there was another record to be sought. Success is fleeting. Every best score can be beaten. High profits can always be higher. But what happens when there are no more conquests to tackle? What do you do when you've reached the top and there's nowhere else to go? This is what happens when you measure what you have achieved in life according to metrics that are determined by *somebody else*. While success has its rewards, those rewards are empty without significance, and the price you pay for success is simply too steep.

Significance Exercise #3: Your Balancing Act

We all balance personal obligations, professional responsibilities, and deep passions such as music, art, or travel. But striking the right balance for significance can be difficult. Are you balancing your life based on your own passions and priorities, or are you directed by the need to please others?

Rate each of the following areas of your life based on your agreement with the following statements. Give yourself one point for each a), two points for each b) and three points for each c).

Questions	I agree...
1. I am able to leave my work at work and not bring it home or on vacation.	a) Not much b) Somewhat c) Completely
2. I make time every day to do something for pure enjoyment.	a) Not much b) Somewhat c) Completely
3. I give my needs as high or higher a priority than the demands of superiors or clients.	a) Not much b) Somewhat c) Completely
4. I take on tasks primarily because I believe in them, not because they make me look good.	a) Not much b) Somewhat c) Completely
5. At day's end, I usually feel there was enough time to finish something that gives me satisfaction.	a) Not much b) Somewhat c) Completely
6. I direct part of my income to causes I care about.	a) Not much b) Somewhat c) Completely
7. I don't feel guilty when I take personal time away from my job.	a) Not much b) Somewhat c) Completely
8. No matter how tired my work makes me, I have something I do that makes me feel recharged.	a) Not much b) Somewhat c) Completely
9. I make a living doing something I love.	a) Not much b) Somewhat c) Completely
10. Some of the people I work with also spend time with me doing things for other people or engaging in something I enjoy.	a) Not much b) Somewhat c) Completely

Scoring

30-36 points: Your life is geared toward self-directed balance and significance.

21-29 points: You're one of the majority who is somewhat in balance but with many areas of life out of balance. You should examine every aspect of your life—work, home, relationships, health, spirituality, dreams—to figure out where you can start to replace others' motivations with your own.

12-20 points: Balance is hard to come by, but stress and dissatisfaction aren't. You should consider systemic changes to your entire life's decision-making process.

The Only Measurement is in the Mirror

You find significance in life when you pursue objectives that are determined by the beliefs, expectations, and requirements of one person: *you*. In order to live up to the expectations of the face you see in the mirror, you must know the person behind that face. What do you stand for? What do you want? What could you spend the rest of your life doing each day and never be bored? Those seem like rudimentary questions, but in reality few of us spend any time considering the answers. We spend our childhood measuring ourselves by the expectations of our parents and teachers. We spend our adolescence and young adulthood measured by the critical eyes of our peers. We spend our adulthood trying to live up to the measure of bosses, spouses, and society at large. Introspection becomes something monks do.

A vital milestone in personal development is stepping back and seeing clearly that rather than blindly chase success for its own sake, it is healthier, wiser, and far more spiritually satisfying to seek significance by becoming involved in activities that align with your passions and beliefs. We all have a yearning to be accepted or needed, to make a difference. But before you can do that, you have to ask those tough questions and take those first steps.

In Central Florida, where Florida's Blood Centers' headquarters are located, a survey on the concept of "Social Capital" and service was conducted while this book was being written. The study showed that of the citizens surveyed, about a quarter of them were volunteering, or participating in service-related activities that were close to their heart, a few times a year. While it's encouraging that there are people out there with a mind for service, this also reveals that 75 percent of the people were doing little to contribute to society outside of their own families. There is plenty of "need" out there, believe me. Take your pick from statistics according to reports:

- More than 37 million people in the United States live in poverty.
- About 862 million people across the world routinely go hungry.
- Nearly a billion people entered the twenty-first century unable to read a book or sign their names.
- The richest 20 percent of the world's population accounts for three-quarters of the world's income.

Some look at these numbers and shrug. Others look and feel overwhelmed. Enlightened individuals see great opportunity to free themselves from the trap of success by directing their passion and talents toward service. The effort might be indirect, or you might be more focused on fulfilling a deep need that has nothing to do with service, such as music, art, writing, or theology. But in the end, if you serve the essence of your being, you will be in a position to inspire, delight, or help others.

Significance Story

A Gift They Won't Forget

Alma Powell, who chairs American's Promise Alliance, a nonprofit organization co-founded in 1997 by her husband, former Secretary of State Colin Powell, recalls a holiday season she spent alone at a new job in Los Angeles, far away from family and friends.

"Rather than indulging in self-pity (an option I seriously considered), I decided to serve turkey dinner to homeless folks on Christmas Eve. It was a heartwarming day. I remember in particular one scruffy young man, all alone and down on his luck, but with eyes agleam as he came back for seconds. "I love the stuffing!" he said with a smile. "Me, too," I said.

This time of year we think a lot about giving; out come the wish lists, followed by the panicked rush to the malls. But here's something to add to the mix: the gift of service, which may well be the best gift of all. "You, through minimal effort, can make a big difference in someone's life," says Alma Powell. "And when you give back to others, you get something back yourself."

—From AARP

Unfortunately, it is almost inevitable that we fall into the "trap of success" at one time or another. After all, it's understandable that at some point in life we're preoccupied with making money, ascending the career ladder and impressing people. But where does it end? It helps to know the signs and symptoms of success obsession or Other-Directed Balance, the "temptations" that can distract us from significance. We all have weaknesses, no matter how virtuous we think we are, and society can make the journey to significance even more turbulent. For an instructive example, let's look at ancient Rome—a society that, despite its potential for significance, plummeted thanks to an insatiable thirst for success and instant gratification.

Rome: A Lesson in the Threats of Success

The sounds of prosperity echoed through the streets. Commerce was at an all-time high. Many citizens were enjoying the good life. The rich had plans to become richer, and even some of the poor began having visions of wealth. Then, in what seemed like the blink of an eye, everything changed.

Thousands of tourists travel around the world each year to visit the ruins of the Roman Empire: the Forum, the Colosseum, the aqueducts. At its zenith, Rome was a continent-spanning republic famed for its intellect; engineers, scholars, statesmen, and philosophers contributed to its remarkable systems of administration, law, economy, art, culture, education, and infrastructure. Several of the emperors leading up to Rome's decline were proponents of civil service, believers in equality, and patrons of the needy and poor. For nearly one thousand years before its fall, Rome was the largest, wealthiest, and most politically significant city in the Western world.

While the reason for Rome's fall is a contentious issue among historians, one might sum up the decay of the great empire by saying this: Rome became so powerful and prosperous, its people lost their focus on the ideals that brought them to greatness. When time and resources gave the emperors and leaders of Rome the opportunity to pursue noble concepts that would benefit the most fragile members of their society, they instead became obsessed with the pursuit of self-gratification: sex, gluttony, slavery. They over-extended the empire's resources in the constant pursuit of conquest into territories they could not sustain, such as Scotland. The foundation of wealth, power, and success could no longer support a society that lacked the soul and will to better mankind as a whole.

Of Rome, Edward Gibbon wrote in his classic *The Decline and Fall of the Roman Empire*:

> *But the decline of Rome was the natural and inevitable effect of immoderate greatness. Prosperity ripened the principle of decay; the causes of destruction multiplied with the extent of conquest; and, as soon as time or accident had removed the artificial supports, the stupendous fabric yielded to the pressure of its own weight. … The victorious legions, who in distant wars acquired the vices of strangers and mercenaries, first oppressed the freedom of the republic, and afterwards violated the majesty of the purple. The emperors, anxious for their personal safety and the public peace, were reduced to the base expedient of corrupting the discipline which rendered them alike formidable to their sovereign and to the enemy; the vigour of the military government was relaxed, and finally dissolved, by the partial institutions of Constantine; and the Roman world was overwhelmed by a deluge of Barbarians.*

Although ours may be a simplistic view of the fall of Rome, it speaks to the idea there were seeds planted along the way that grew into vines that strangled the great society. Other cultures have followed the same pattern from altruism and service to self-indulgence and decadence. China was a great source for discovery and creativity, but constrained by the repression of totalitarianism and Communism, its creative fires have been stamped out. Like Egypt and Rome in ancient times, China was a country that did great things when it had a focus on significance. When it became self-absorbed and greedy, it fell from grace.

So what about the United States in these times? Are we on the same path as Rome? Look at the facts:

- We live in the most powerful society in history.
- We have wealth beyond the dreams of our ancestors.
- We have more opportunity to pursue ideas and compassion for others, but we are constantly under pressure to pursue wealth, goods, and success.
- We allow millions in our society to live in poverty, without healthcare and suffering from crime and illiteracy.

Are we planting the seeds of a noxious crop that will choke our society? Certainly, the messages we send through the media are all screaming, "Consume! Attain! Multitask!" We can turn on the television at any time and see people in constant pursuit of self-gratification, with constant pressure from cultural icons and advertisers to chase after the latest expensive toys under the delusion that they will bring us happiness. Meanwhile, others struggle to put food on the table or pay bills to even turn on their lights. We hunt for success while many ignore significance.

The Roman Empire grew beyond its ability to serve its people, and its foundations were torn away as the discipline of a younger empire became consumed with less-noble pursuits. Our society has some indicators of the same thing that warrant watching. While it is easy to point fingers at government, we must remember our nation was declared a nation of the people, by the people, and for the people. Until we as individuals take notice and begin to pull the weeds of selfishness from our society, we will be in jeopardy of a great fall.

Symptoms That You're On the Wrong Path

The only religion that ought to be taught is the religion of fearlessness.
—*Swami Vivekananda, Hindu missionary*

The quote from Lord Acton is, "Power corrupts, and absolute power corrupts absolutely." Maybe, but I think it's more relevant for our society to say desire corrupts. The pursuit of success, the influence of money and power, and lack of consideration for the common man, have led many down a path of crime and corruption. We read about them so often that the following headlines, found while I was working on this book, tell a disturbingly accurate story of our society:

"Illinois Governor Rod Blagojevich Arrested On Corruption Charges"
"Banks Fear Huge Losses in Madoff Ponzi Scheme"
"KB Home Executive Agrees to Guilty Plea in Backdating Scandal"
"German electronics company Siemens Pays $1.4 Billion in Bribery Settlement"
"Chinese Crackdown Finds 36 Basketball Players Gave False Ages"

The pattern is clear: When people yield to the temptation to pursue shallow, material rewards by any means necessary, they not only damage their own spirits and sicken their morals, they harm society as a whole. The good news is that it is possible to resist this tide by focusing your energies on compassion, good works, and reaching out to others, and on the passions that glow from the deepest recesses of your being. Millions of people do just that; they are community activists, volunteers, artists, hospice workers, musicians, teachers' aides … the list is long and hopeful. But you must make the choice to reject the easy, quick pursuit of material success to focus on significance.

> **Balance:** *The bargain in which the pursuit of wealth and position shares time and energy equally with helping others, pursuing personal passions, and creating a legacy.*

How do you know if you're balancing your desire for success with your mission to create significance and meaning in your life? Well, if you hate your job and barely have time to breathe or see your children, you already know, but most of us aren't like that. Even if we are severely out of balance and dedicate most of our hours to climbing the corporate ladder and padding our bank accounts, we're often numb to the bigger picture. We have our noses pressed so firmly to the grindstone that we can't lift our heads to look around. But fortunately, there are symptoms that you are heading down a path which will lead to alienation, regret, and emptiness:

Fear—This is man's greatest enemy, and it manifests itself in forms as diverse as shame, jealousy, anger, insolence, and arrogance. It breeds distrust, misunderstandings, conflict, and corruption. In its pure form, fear is a survival mechanism. But for some, fear becomes the driving force in their lives: fear of loss, of not fitting in, of abandonment, of falling behind some societal norm for wealth and power. Fear distorts our thinking and compels us to make choices we would not otherwise make.

My son, whose father is Egyptian, lives every day with the fear of what others may do to someone with Middle Eastern heritage. Young people who came of age after watching the planes fly into the World Trade Center buildings saw the faces of the people responsible and saw faces that resemble that of my son. Fear poisons everything, and if you find yourself motivated by fear, then you are probably on the path to success but little significance. The causes are many—disconnection or misunderstanding of others, lack of confidence, living selfishly instead of living in part for your community—but until you make the choice to overcome them, fear will continue to block your ability to be significant.

Rampant Consumerism—I am blessed to live in the United States, where capitalism and a free market can flourish. That freedom provides unprecedented opportunities to discover new solutions and provides all people with a chance to prosper. But with freedom comes responsibility. Sometimes, instead of taking advantage of the opportunities of a free-market society, we find ourselves being taken advantage of.

Rampant consumerism is a voracious appetite for the acquisition of possessions and the pursuit of pleasure through wealth. We are bombarded each day with messages telling us that in order to "measure up," we must buy the latest and greatest televisions, cars, boats, clothes. Even our children are prey to an endless stream of advertising. They become conditioned to the lie that by consuming an endless stream of material things, they will find greater happiness. Sadly, we know this is not the case. Consumerism in its most virulent form is addictive, with one purchase providing a temporary "high" that fades, compelling the consumer to buy more. Left unchecked, this programming produces adults who cannot be satisfied, driven to fill the emptiness of their lives with material goods instead of relationships, generosity, spirituality, and creativity.

Our society has taught us we should "have it all," and that having it all will help feed and sustain us. But somehow, even with everything we have, we still aren't happy. I have seen children in other parts of the world who have nothing jump and play in the polluted waters of the Nile. They seemed just as joyful as the children of this country who play on beautiful beaches. I have watched the elderly gather to play cards or enjoy one another's company in the town centers in Portugal. They, too, appeared to find pleasure in simple pastimes. It has occurred to me that the "scarcity" in these people's lives is an illusion. They are rich in what is important to them: relationships with others, time to enjoy life, peace, and delight. They don't care about having a new plasma TV or an iPod. When you don't feel pressured to "have it all," you learn to treasure what you do have and appreciate the things money and power can't buy.

In many of our lives, however, consumerism has blurred the line between need and want. It has created a society of people who find it impossible to be content and must acquire more to find happiness. Take the example of Randy from the first chapter. He was making a large salary, his kids were in the right schools and he owned a boat—and he was miserable. Being a super-consumer was not satisfying to his true, inner self, which is why he lit up after giving blood.

Do you feel pressured to be an obsessive consumer? Have you racked up massive debt buying things you don't use or don't even want? Are you working to support your stuff with no time for yourself? Those are more symptoms that your scale is tipped toward success and away from significance.

Technological Isolation—The idea of technology uniting us is wonderful in theory, but in practice it has bred a tribalism that didn't really exist before the Internet. The explosion of millions of Web sites, chat rooms, and virtual communities has spawned a subculture of people who are perfectly comfortable with the solitude of living life on the Web, never having to interact in person, and never coming into contact with opinions that are different from their own.

The 1995 movie *The Net*, starring Sandra Bullock, depicted the life of such a woman. Her identity and her life were lived behind a monitor. No one really knew her. When her identity was stolen, she had no one to come to her defense. Even her neighbors could not recognize her. It may be Hollywood drama, but there are Web sites and social networks where people create identities based on who they would like to be. Their "friends" are virtual and they live in a digital reality where no one connects in the real world.

Technology also gives us the potential to be "always on." There are people who are always connected, always reachable by cell phone, e-mail, or text message. Unless we can unplug and turn off our electronic devices, there is no space for solitude or quiet self-reflection. If you're taking your cell phone on vacation, are you really on vacation? More to the point, if you aren't taking time to really tune into yourself, to figure out who you really are, how can you expect anyone else to know you? The "connectedness" created by technology frequently has the effect of isolating us and enabling our obsession with work, success, and material gain. Are you someone who is tethered to Facebook or your iPhone twenty-four hours a day? You may be showing another sign of being out of balance.

It is nearly impossible to gain the self-knowledge needed for significance when you are primarily driven by these three forces:

1. Self-gratification and selfishness, trying to attain "items" you identify as measurements of your worth.
2. Desire for the approval of others.
3. The message that if you do not measure up to society's expectations, you are a failure.

When We Get *Significancer*

When we don't measure up, we find coping mechanisms. Some look to food, and as a result we have become the "supersize me" nation. Obesity is at an all-time high, leading to record highs of diabetes, heart disease, and stroke. It is difficult to strive for significance when poor health imprisons you.

Others cope by going into debt. They must live at the right address, so they take on unsustainable mortgages of the kind that have helped bring down our economy in the last year. And if they are living in the house, they simply *must* live the lifestyle. As a result, carrying twenty-thousand dollars in credit card debt with zero savings is almost a badge of honor.

These conditions lead to mental or emotional problems that often result in self-destructive or relationship-sabotaging behavior. I call them *significancer*, because they dominate our minds and make striving for self-knowledge and a broader spiritual mission almost impossible. Stress, depression, addiction, abuse, and divorce are the inevitable result of the symptoms discussed earlier, and they are part of a vicious cycle: When your life is miserable and desperate, you're so busy trying to survive, you can't take the time to figure out what went wrong and how to change it. Significancer is one of the most important concepts in the subject of significance, and we're going to talk about it quite a lot—what it is, how to recognize it, and how to beat it.

> *Significancer: A disease of significance, in which we compensate for the emptiness and meaninglessness of our lives by escaping into mindless pleasures or destructive behaviors.*

Significance Exercise #4: Significancer Screening

When we have significancer, it's often easier to cope through escaping than to face the painful, challenging work of changing our lives. What methods are you using to compensate for your deviation from a significant path? Complete the exercise and get your diagnosis.

Rate your activity in each of the following areas of life on a scale of one to ten, with one being that you never engage in the activity, ten being that you engage in it almost every day.

I drink to excess.

  1   2   3   4   5   6   7   8   9   10

I use illegal or prescription drugs.

  1   2   3   4   5   6   7   8   9   10

I spend excessively and run up large debts.

  1   2   3   4   5   6   7   8   9   10

I falsify work or steal from my employer.

  1   2   3   4   5   6   7   8   9   10

I eat to excess.

  1   2   3   4   5   6   7   8   9   10

I spend many hours on the Internet.

  1   2   3   4   5   6   7   8   9   10

I cheat on my significant other.

  1   2   3   4   5   6   7   8   9   10

I dive into my work, often working sixty hours a week or more.

  1   2   3   4   5   6   7   8   9   10

Scoring

8-20 points: You show no signs of significancer. You are well on your way to a significant, meaningful life.

21-40 points: You have some significancer risk factors. It would be wise to examine aspects of your life that are leaving you feeling empty and unfulfilled and make some changes.

41-60 points: You have early stage significancer, but treatment such as pursuing passions, reinventing your career or helping others can drive it into remission.

61-80 points: You have advanced significancer. If you don't make major changes soon, it may be too late to live the life you once dreamed of.

Significancer is preventable. We can look back in history and find warnings against excess and encouragement to find our true selves in non-material pursuits. The Seven Deadly Sins exist as a warning that excessive concern over accumulation of things will never fill deeper, more spiritual needs. Indian political and spiritual leader Mohandas Gandhi had his own take on the Seven Deadly Sins and how they play out in our daily actions. They are:

- Wealth without work
- Pleasure without conscience
- Science without humanity
- Knowledge without character
- Politics without principle
- Commerce without mortality
- Worship without sacrifice

Sound familiar? All of these qualities are alive and well in our society. Why? In part, because we see our current situation as beyond change. But a person seeking significance does not view life as a hopeless cause. As you begin to tilt your balance more toward the search for significance, you remove your rose-colored glasses, examine reality and begin a quest to change the direction of your life, your community, even your society. Even a single, small match can give light to a darkened cave. If we each begin to pursue significance and light the darkness in our corner of the world, the collective glow can be seen in society to light the path and enable us to step over the temptations seeded along the way.

An old axiom states, "There are three kinds of people. First, those who make things happen. Second, those who watch things happen. And third, those who say, 'What happened?'" The journey called life seldom allows time for reflection to piece together who we really are and who we are called to become. But to fulfill our lives to the utmost, we must look inside, learn about ourselves, and live according to our passions and principles, not according to the expectations of others. Real satisfaction comes from pairing our own ambitions with a higher calling.

REFLECTION

Consider the common axiom "Those who don't learn from history are doomed to repeat it." Great time and effort has been put into the study of past and potential falls of countries, rulers, and nations, resulting in many theories about what causes social and moral decline. Think about your own life: What vices or "sins" do you commit that can be weeded out to help you reach and stay at the peak of your significance?

Next Steps for Significance Seekers...

- *... Interview the three most materially successful people you know about their lives.*

- *... Interview the three most spiritually or compassionately significant people you know about their lives.*

- *... Compare the two sets of interviews. What patterns do you see?*

- *... Make a personal timeline of your life, tracking key "decision points" when you had to choose one path or another. What drove your decisions at each point? Dreams? Money? Someone's expectations?*

- *... Make a personal balance sheet with two columns: "Want" and "Obligation." Then for one week, keep track of the things you do because you want to do them and the things you do because you feel obligated. Then contrast the two lists.*

- *... Ask, "What is my true calling in this life?"*

CHAPTER THREE
The Journey To Significance

THE IMPORTANCE OF INTROSPECTION AND CANDID SELF-EVALUATION AS PART OF THE PROCESS OF DISCOVERING A PATH TO SIGNIFICANCE

> *It is good to have an end to journey toward, but it is the journey that matters in the end.*
>
> —*Ursula K. LeGuin, science fiction writer*

The seeker of success and the seeker of significance have different journeys. The success seeker's journey is based solely on manufacturing outside appearances and accomplishments which help that person meet the expectations of others. I describe this as being a journey of *acquisition*, in which the focus is to gather more and more things and positions while remaining the same person inside. When you are seeking success for its own sake in this way, the journey is just a means to an end, and you will not appreciate your surroundings or the journey itself. In driving hard for your destination, you miss the scenery.

A significance seeker's journey is based on a deep understanding of his or her being and the things that he or she was put here to achieve. It is a *transformational* journey. The journey is the reward in itself because the whole goal is for the person to undergo meaningful, positive change—mentally, emotionally, and spiritually. The trip is based on a drive to accomplish more than mere success by positively affecting and encouraging others on their own journeys, to help others transform their lives and themselves. The significance seeker acknowledges and appreciates the journey and cherishes the sights seen and lessons learned while on it.

Proud Mary

Some years ago, I was walking out the doors of the Florida's Blood Centers office in downtown Orlando and ran into a woman named Mary. She was a bit older than me and she walked with that great strength and confidence I envy. I hadn't noticed it at first, but we had started walking together as she came out of the donor room and I was coming from my office. My mind was racing with the many items on my "to do" list. I was trying to do everything, build my place in the organization and achieve so many things, and the pressure was overwhelming that afternoon. I remember catching Mary out of the corner of my eye because she was trying to keep her two young sons in line as they headed to the door. They were dressed up like they had just come from church or a party and were a bit rambunctious.

Mary and I arrived at the exit doors together, and I tried to hold the door so she could manage with the children. She and the kids thanked me and we introduced ourselves. Then I asked the same question I ask everyone I meet coming out of the blood bank: "So, what made you donate blood today?" As the sales and marketing executive, I always wanted to know what motivated donors to make that crucial decision. This time, however, I wasn't prepared for the answer, nor was I prepared for Mary to challenge my thinking and change my life forever.

She stopped and slowly turned. My question had caught her off-guard. She gently corralled the two boys and smiled. "Well, I just came from my mother's funeral," she said without hesitation. "I left the cemetery and drove straight here. It seemed like the right thing to do." Time seemed to stop; her words rang in my head. I had never heard that answer. Mary could see I was shaken, so she reached out and placed her hand on mine and went on. "You see, my mother instilled in me when I was very young that our lives were meant to share with others, and that sometimes, we must dig deeper when we are hurting to do something for someone else who may be hurting more."

She smiled again, and as she turned to walk away, all I could say as my eyes welled up was a weak, "Thank you." My pressing to-do list dissolved into one clear thought: *That is the most significant act I have ever heard of.* Mary had done so much with one simple gesture. She had passed on her mother's legacy of wisdom, given a lifesaving gift to someone she did not know, delivered a powerful lesson for her two young children, and inspired a busy young executive trying to conquer the world. I was in awe.

This experience inspired my lifelong passion for profiling blood donors. They amaze me. I wanted to know what makes them tick. After meeting Mary, I wondered, what did she get out of her donation that day? Why did she put aside her own grief in order to help others? My experience with Mary, and many other amazing people I have met through my years in the blood banking industry, ignited a desire to understand the inner lives of my fellow travelers.

We all have things we must do, responsibilities we have to fulfill. But what helps us overcome our own daily hardships to make a difference in one life or one hundred lives? How does a person evolve to a state in which he or she puts compassion, healing, and understanding above everything else?

I think psychologist Abraham Maslow's Hierarchy of Needs offers true insight here. I think he and I would agree on what makes people like Mary tick: *the drive to be significant.*

Designed for Significance

Maslow's work in the 1940s still stands as one of the most revered theories about human behavior. His Hierarchy of Needs demonstrates the steps we take toward *self-actualization* and becoming secure and comfortable with who we are. Self-actualization leads us to a place where we can give more of ourselves and impact others for good. His premise is that once our basic human needs are met, we progress and grow toward new levels of being or significance. Ideally, these needs are met as we progress in age. However, there are situations that occur in life that cause us to regress and fall back down to the more basic levels of the hierarchy. His basic needs were called deficit needs, all leading to the *being needs* of self-actualization.

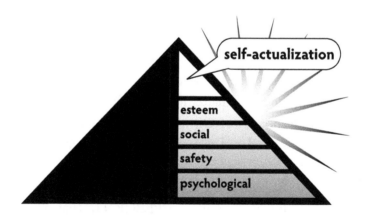

Dr. C. George Boeree recaps Maslow's hierarchy this way:

1. **The physiological needs**. These include the needs we have for oxygen, water, protein, salt, sugar, calcium, and other minerals and vitamins. They also include the need to maintain a pH balance and temperature (98.6 or near to it). Also, there are the needs to be active, to rest, to sleep, to get rid of wastes, to avoid pain, and to have sex.

2. **The safety and security needs**. When the physiological needs are largely taken care of, this second layer of needs comes into play. You become increasingly interested in finding safe circumstances, stability, and protection.

3. **The love and belonging needs**. When physiological needs and safety needs are, by and large, taken care of, a third layer starts to show up. You begin to feel the need for friends, a sweetheart, children, affectionate relationships in general, and even a sense of community.

4. **The esteem needs**. Next, we begin to look for self-esteem. Maslow noted two versions of esteem needs: lower and higher. The lower level is the need for the respect of others, for status, fame, glory, recognition, attention, reputation, appreciation, dignity, or even dominance. The higher form involves the need for self-respect, including such feelings as confidence, competence, achievement, mastery, independence, and freedom.

5. **The self-actualization needs.** The last level is different from the others. Maslow has used a variety of terms to refer to this level, calling it ***growth motivation, being needs, or self-actualization***. These are needs that do not involve balance. Once engaged, they continue to be felt. In fact, they are likely to become stronger as we "feed" them. They involve the continuous desire to fulfill potentials, to "be all that you can be." They are a matter of becoming the most complete, the fullest "you"—hence the term self-actualization.

Part of Maslow's research included a collection of biographical profiles of individuals he considered to be achievers of the self-actualization level, including Abraham Lincoln, Thomas Jefferson, Albert Einstein, Eleanor Roosevelt, Jane Adams, William James, Albert Schweitzer, Benedict Spinoza, and Aldous Huxley. These are not bad footsteps to follow if you are on a journey toward significance.

Maslow's study of self-actualization led him to believe only 2 percent of the population was operating at a level of self-actualization ... 2 PERCENT. That means the rest of us are striving somewhere below, still trying to figure out who we are and what we need. Imagine the possibilities if more people began to seek self-actualization, to become significant by maximizing their potential for giving, creating, and healing. How could we change the world?

Another truth about significance many people miss is that significant acts do not have to be world-shaking. You don't have to be Bill Gates curing HIV in Africa, or Brad Pitt building homes for victims of Hurricane Katrina. Significance has nothing whatsoever to do with your acts being grand or publicized or affecting the lives of millions. In reality, an act need only meet two criteria to be significant:

1. It must touch and change at least one person from the inside out, giving that person or persons beauty, hope, love, security, health, or knowledge, for example.
2. It must reflect the essence of the kind of being you aspire to become—your highest, best purpose, without consideration for career or income.

Under these criteria, a grandmother who gives fifty dollars a month from her Social Security check to an organization that makes micro-loans to help women in Third World countries start businesses and feed their families is significant. A corporate CEO who runs a $30 billion company and lives in a mansion but never sees his kids and ravages the environment is not significant. In our society, one is completely anonymous while the other enjoys the prestige and admiration of society. That's the focus of our culture. As the paradigm shifts, we must redefine greatness and turn self-actualized people into our role models, the people who get the headlines. Wouldn't that be refreshing?

Significance Exercise #5: Your Hierarchy of Needs

How well have you addressed each of Maslow's core needs in your own life? Time to find out.

First, for each of the Maslow needs, describe how you have addressed it to date. Then rate your satisfaction of each need on a scale of one to ten. No scoring here; just insight into how you're meeting the most essential needs of human existence.

---

1. **Physiological Needs (food, sex, sleep, etc.)**

Not met   1   2   3   4   5   6   7   8   9   10   **Completely Met**

---

2. **Security Needs (income, physical shelter, healthcare, etc.)**

Not met   1   2   3   4   5   6   7   8   9   10   **Completely Met**

---

3. **Love and Belonging Needs**

Not met   1   2   3   4   5   6   7   8   9   10   **Completely Met**

---

4. **Esteem Needs (respect of others, self-respect)**

Not met   1   2   3   4   5   6   7   8   9   10   **Completely Met**

---

5. **Self-Actualization Needs (personal potential, fulfillment, growth)**

Not met   1   2   3   4   5   6   7   8   9   10   **Completely Met**

Significance Story

How often in life do we see something on TV or on the street and think, "That's not fair," or "What a shame"? But how often do we do something about it? While awareness is an important step in the process, seeking significance also requires a desire to "repair" those injustices or alleviate the anguish around you.

Maybe you think you don't have the power to fix a serious problem. But your contribution counts. While one man might not be able to move a boulder, ten men (or women) can. Not all of them become famous, and none of them can do it alone. But each one has the desire to repair what they see as injustice.

Take, for instance, Laura Clay. While not as well-known as some of the more famous suffragettes like Susan B. Anthony, she was a leader in the movement, dedicating her life to women's rights. Her parents divorced and her mother was left homeless because, back then, women didn't have rights to the division of assets or child support. Recognizing this injustice, Clay committed her life to repairing it through serving the cause of women's rights.

Along with hundreds of other women, she tirelessly lobbied for reforms like protection of women's wages and property, the right for women to make wills and contracts, and the ability to control real estate. She helped enact laws in her state to increase the age of consent for females, and allow enrollment for women in male schools. Clay was even the first woman to have her name placed for nomination for president of the United States, opening the door for the thousands of women today who have found their passion in a career in politics.

Why did Clay do these things? She identified injustice and sought to remedy it. She had the passion and the courage to stand up for what she thought was right and fight for it, even in the face of adversity. She chose a path of significance. Each of us has the ability to make positive change. What's most important to remember is that many of the most significant things we can do happen in the smallest and most private moments when we lift up others from the depths of despair.

The Significant Seven

You'll notice that when I talk about the traits people of significance possess, they all come in lists of seven. Why? Well, believe it or not, while the length of these lists started as coincidence, there is actually a significant meaning behind the number itself. The number seven is strongly associated with the Bible. In the Bible, numbers have spiritual significance. Of all the numbers in this sacred book, seven has the most substantial implications, and is used almost six hundred times. In the Bible, seven stands for "spiritual perfection" and is most often cited from this famous passage in Genesis 2:

> *Thus the heavens and the earth were finished, and all the host of them. And on the seventh day God ended His work which He had made; and He rested on the seventh day from all His work which He had made. And God blessed the seventh day, and sanctified it: because that in it He had rested from all His work which God created and made.*

Even outside of the Bible, the number seven is associated with totality and completeness. The Hebrew word for seven comes from the root "savah," which means to be "complete" or "satisfied." The study of numerology, which is based on the belief that there is a relationship between numbers and living things, says the number seven is "the number of completeness" and is linked to stability, balance, and immortality. It is a number of healing and miracles, faith, and dreams come true.

Whether you adhere to a religion or not, the number seven can be seen as a stamp that constitutes a complete cycle. I hope the lessons presented in sets of seven in this book will help you carry out a cycle within yourself, a cycle for fulfillment and completeness that is experienced when you seek significance.

"Significance seekers" share these Seven Pillars of Personal Development:

1. Discernment. These people have a strong ability to discern the genuine from the fake in the people around them. The ability to see the truth about others comes from being familiar with their own image in the mirror. They are accustomed to being brutally honest and measuring their own progress against the internal yardstick of their core beliefs. When you have spent enough time identifying your own emerging superficiality, you easily recognize it in others. This ability helps significance seekers recognize the motivations of others and align themselves with those who seek what they seek.

2. Activism. They see problems or injustice and take action to change the situation. They do not dwell on an issue. They take the challenges life presents and develop a plan to meet them. Significance seekers don't always have an easy life. On the contrary; some of their most significant moments have come during great trials. People of significance take negative situations and use them to become wiser and stronger. They do not allow defeat and disappointment to have the final say.

3. Reflection. They appreciate the journey. They realize that in life, the end may not always justify the means, and that sometimes it is the journey toward a goal that becomes the goal. We rush through so much of life and miss the view along the way. For example, something sad happened in America with the development of the interstate highway system. We lost the desire to make stops along the way. Our focus has become getting to the destination. This literal transportation view mirrors our lives. We are focused on achieving status and accumulating more, and while there is nothing wrong with success, we have distorted it to become the be-all and end-all of our lives. When many people reach the pinnacle of their success, they are empty. They never learned to be significant along the way so they can eventually enjoy the view from the top. Often, once they get there, it's too late to change anything.

4. Self-Esteem. Significance seekers are able to admit to and accept their own shortcomings because they fully recognize and value those things at which they show genius. They are not boastful, but they know what they do well, know how their strengths can enhance a situation, and will not shy away from taking a leadership position when they know they are the most qualified or skilled person on the scene. They know and love who they are and what they are becoming.

5. Principles. Significant people operate from a strong core of beliefs and ethics that prevent them from being swayed by the winds of trends. They allow their moral, ethical, and spiritual beliefs to draw lines in the sand in the desert of compromise. They will not allow pressures or expectations from society to keep them from their life mission, even if that hampers their temporary success.

6. Humility. Significance Seekers are not about themselves. They seek to serve others. They are able to look at a person's strengths, assess their own weak areas, and partner with others in order to accomplish more than either could alone. Ego does not stand in the way of achievement. They are not ashamed or embarrassed to verbalize weakness or fear, knowing it can lead to support and solutions. They ask for help because they are aware of but not afraid of their own shortcomings, and they give others the security and freedom to admit their weaknesses so everyone can work through issues together in a way that leads to positive outcomes. They are able to have conversations and make the person they are speaking with feel like the only one in the room. Our society tends to downplay humility, believing it makes us doormats. That could not be further from the truth. True humility says, "I am worthy because I value and acknowledge the worth of others."

7. Mindfulness. Significant people laugh ... a lot! They have learned life is short and we need to enjoy it along the way. They bring energy into a room through their positive presence. They find joy in the simple beauties of life. They pause for sunsets, anticipate the dawn and dance in the rain, laugh over spilled milk and cry for the broken-hearted. They have learned through experience that people are the priorities, and that projects will get accomplished when people are working as a team. People of significance bring those teams together with a positive, joyful outlook on life.

> *Significance Seeker: Someone on the path to significance through rigorous self-knowledge and the development of the Seven Pillars.*

Significance Exercise #6: The Seven Pillars

How many of the Seven Pillars have you developed to a significant level? This exercise will reveal much about your personal self-evolution ... and show you how far you have to go to reach your potential.

This isn't a test you take yourself; you're not objective about your own development, after all. Instead, ask three people who know you well (and who can be honest) to rate you on each of the Seven Pillars on a scale of one to ten. Be sure to explain each Pillar clearly to them. Average the three scores for each Key for a good idea of where you stand.

Discernment	Activism	Reflection
First person's rating:	First person's rating:	First person's rating:
Second person's rating:	Second person's rating:	Second person's rating:
Third person's rating:	Third person's rating:	Third person's rating:
Average of the three:	Average of the three:	Average of the three:
_____	_____	_____
Self-Esteem	**Principles**	**Humility**
First person's rating:	First person's rating:	First person's rating:
Second person's rating:	Second person's rating:	Second person's rating:
Third person's rating:	Third person's rating:	Third person's rating:
Average of the three:	Average of the three:	Average of the three:
_____	_____	_____

Mindfulness	Scoring (your average for each Pillar)
First person's rating:	8-10: This Pillar is extremely well-developed. You don't need to worry about working on it as you go forward, just maintaining your excellence.
Second person's rating:	
Third person's rating:	5-7: You're above average in this area, but some concerted effort toward change would bring you great joy and meaning.
Average of the three:	1-4: Your life is being stunted somewhat by your poor performance in this area. Bringing up this average score should become a major goal in the future.
_____	

If there is a figure in modern history who exemplified these qualities, it would be Mother Teresa of Calcutta. Recognized and respected worldwide as a humanitarian, she was an advocate for the poor, helpless, and unwanted for nearly fifty years. Though she took her first religious vows as a nun named Agnes Gonxha Bojaxhiu in 1931, it is said Mother Teresa first received what she explained as "the call within the call" in 1946, which compelled her to begin missionary work with the poor and to begin living among the most impoverished people on earth.

To help fulfill her calling, Mother Teresa received Vatican permission to found the Missionaries of Charity in Calcutta, India, in 1950. Over the years, as her message of charity, kindness, and selflessness spread, the order and various other organizations established by Mother Teresa attracted recruits and contributions of service and money. Mother Teresa's mission for significance had a resonance so strong that what started as a small society of thirteen members in 1950 has grown into an international network of organizations composed of roughly 450 brothers, 5,000 nuns, and 100,000 volunteers operating 600 missions, schools, and shelters in 120 countries.

Though she passed away in 1997, Mother Teresa left a legacy that lives on, and her compassion resonates today through the efforts of others who are following in her footsteps. Mother Teresa once said, "Good works are links that form a chain of love." If you wish to be significant, be not just a link but a strong and compelling link so your chain or legacy can continue to live on as hers has.

REFLECTION

Which of the seven qualities of significance do you possess and which do you need to improve on? What needs in your life are being met and what moves do you need to make to propel yourself toward "self-actualization" or significance?

The Choice

In a world that demands so much of our time and energy, how do we become significant? Quite simply, we *choose* to do so. Are you willing to make the choice for significance? It's not any easy decision, and it demands a change in thinking. This is not a fad diet along the buffet of life. It is a new way to open a menu of possibilities for not only yourself, but for those around you. However, it demands permanent changes in your thinkingówhat you see as your obligations to others and to yourself, what you gauge your own success by, and how you allocate your time. It is easy to spend the majority of our lives spinning on a hamster wheel and fulfilling the destiny of others without regard for who we were intended to be, ignoring the mark we were destined to leave upon this world. Will your mark be one that leaves a path for others to follow toward their own fulfillment? Or, when your time on earth is through, will the world collectively say "The end"?

If you have chosen to seek significance, congratulations! The first step is definition: You must define who you are. Not who you want people to think you are. Who. You. Are. Only then can you begin to assemble the pieces that will make you complete.

Next Steps for Significance Seekers...

- *... Gauge your discernment by observing someone you know well and deducing what kind of day he or she is having.*

- *... Gauge your activism by developing a new product, method, or service to solve a longstanding problem in your organization.*

- *... Gauge your reflection by keeping a "moments journal" for one day and writing down the times when you stop to savor the moment.*

- *... Gauge your self-esteem by asking someone you know well to tell you your greatest weakness or shortcoming. How do you react?*

- *... Gauge your principles by writing down the times in the last five years when you went against your code. What happened? Was the result positive for you?*

- *... Gauge your humility by apologizing without qualification to three people who have it coming. How does that make you feel?*

- *... Gauge your mindfulness by having your kids make a list of the ten things they are grateful for. Make your own list. Then compare them. Should you be mindful and grateful for something else?*

CHAPTER FOUR
Significance is Universal

THE CONCEPT OF SIGNIFICANCE AS VIEWED THROUGH THE WORLD'S MAJOR SPIRITUAL TRADITIONS, WHERE IT IS A UNIVERSAL IDEA

Be faithful in small things because it is in them that your strength lies.
—Mother Teresa of Calcutta, missionary and humanitarian

Hope, selflessness, and compassion are driving forces for those who find significance. They are also consistent and redeeming aspects of many of the great world religions. While this book is not intended to be a study on religions, it is helpful to reflect on some of the beliefs we find at their core to see that the pursuit of significance is a universal truth that stretches all the way back to our origins.

If you were to examine the world's religions, you would find that each one has unique traditions and interpretations of the nature of existence, but all of them generally revolve around recognizing common cycles of life—birth, growth, living, union, enlightenment, service, death, grief, rebirth. All religions are human constructs that we use to lend form and structure to the ineffable, and they reflect the culture and times of their creation and their growth. Religion is a model for significance, because it directs the attention of the devotee inward, toward growth and self-awareness, and outward, toward kindness to fellow men. Each religion, regardless of its creeds or dogma, focuses on self-improvement through both introspection and an awareness of the needs of others. As you review the religions covered in this chapter, I think you will agree that, while different in many aspects, they share common principles, which boil down to:

- Love others.
- Serve others.
- Share wealth with the needy.
- Treat others with respect.
- Build family.
- Respect life.
- Protect the weak.
- Seek peace and justice.

Think about your own beliefs and ambitions. I am willing to bet there are others out there who share your same ideals. It might surprise you which people, even if completely different from you externally, are tied to you through an internal desire or common cause. As you explore these different faith traditions, you will see how similar we all are when we commit to a collective faith in significance, because we are pursuing a universal truth.

Universal truth: Something that is fact for all human beings regardless of age, race, religion, ethnic background, location, economic status, or political belief.

Significance Exercise #7: Your Universal Truths

Most of us hold fast to some core truths. These can be moral codes, beliefs about existence, or spiritual ideas that have nothing to do with organized religion. What are your universal truths?

In each space, describe one of your universal truths (example: "All people deserve equal opportunity in life"), then describe how it affects your behavior and choices.

My universal truth:

How it affects my behavior and choices:

My universal truth:

How it affects my behavior and choices:

My universal truth:

How it affects my behavior and choices:

My universal truth:

How it affects my behavior and choices:

Judaism

Judaism is one of the oldest religions in practice. The history and principles of this religion have influenced other faiths, including Christianity and Islam. Throughout their long history, people of the Jewish faith, like those of most every other religious devotion, have experienced and overcome slavery, persecution, discrimination, conquest, inter-religion conflict, occupation, and exile.

Many Jews follow a set of practices known as "halakhah," which is often translated as "Jewish Law," but literally, and appropriately, translates to "the path one walks." This is evidence that no matter one's faith or convictions, there is always a pathway to significance that begins with adherence to a set of beliefs.

One major element of Jewish law, and of finding significance, relates to the relationship between human beings. Jewish law commands Jews to have compassion for both fellow Jews and strangers—to give "tzedakah," or charity to the needy, and to avoid wronging their fellow man in words or actions. These ideals of compassion and kindness are so ingrained in the Jewish faith that the Jewish word for commandment, "mitzvah," is often used in conversation to refer to any good deed. Here are some specific principles that come straight from this Jewish law that fall right in line with living a significant life:

- Not to stand by idly when a human life is in danger.
- To relieve a neighbor of his burden and help to unload his beast.
- To leave the unreaped corner of the field or orchard for the poor.
- To give charity according to one's means.

Core Values

- Love God.
- Be thy brother's keeper.
- Be everyone's neighbor.
- God shows mercy, justice, and compassion.

- Strive for an ethical life of the highest order—traditions, sharing the bounty, teaching children, controlling harsh words, making life sacred.

Expressions of a Universal Truth

The doctrines of Christians and Jews are the closest of all the world's religions. ... Both are narrative religions. Both are religions of The Book. Both religions teach respect for this world, for the flesh, for the concrete. Both religions instruct their members in a vocation not merely to escape from this world but to change this world. Both find the historical task of modernization a challenge, yet a challenge to be taken up in faith and in hope. ... Both have a commitment to intellect in its rational and scientific parts as well as its mystical, poetic, and intuitive parts.

—Michael Novak, author, philosopher, and theologian

In Judaism we are commanded to "tikkun olam," repair the world. It seems like an impossible task. ... You are God's agent. The first step in "tikkun olam" is "tikkun bayit." Literally, repairing your house. When you heal your home, yourself, you are beginning to change the whole world.

—Sherre Hirsch, rabbi and author

Significance Story

You always hear people talking about "good Samaritans." Many children are told the parable of the "Good Samaritan" when growing up and learning about religion or morals. But do you know the story's true significance?

In modern teachings, the story is often used to exemplify that people should always exhibit kindness and compassion for their neighbors. Much of the story's context has been lost, however, with many people unaware of the religious and ethnic truths it was originally meant to illustrate.

In this story, a Jewish man is beaten, robbed, and left to die on the side of the road by a gang of thieves. Three people end up seeing the man as he lies there half-dead. A priest sees the man and crosses the road to pass him by. A second man, who is a "Levite" of the same Jewish tribe as the dying man, also sees him and continues walking by. Finally, a third man, a Samaritan, sees the man and takes pity on him, bandaging and clothing him, and taking him to a nearby inn, where he pays for the keeper to care for him.

The important point of the story is not merely that the third man had the most compassion, but that the Samaritans were a people who had been oppressed by the Jews. Despite this, the third man set aside any differences or discrimination to show kindness for a fellow human being.

This story is a perfect example of what this chapter hopes to teach. The parable of the Samaritan shows there exists an inherent quality that goes beyond color, ethnicity, or religion. There is a universal moral law, a collective truth that people of significance live by to guide their every idea and action.

Significance Icon

Abraham, the biblical patriarch, is seen as one of the physical and spiritual ancestors of Judaism, as well as the first to give expression to the Jewish faith. The son of an idol merchant, Abraham questioned the faith of his father from an early age and constantly sought truth. He believed the entire universe was the work of a single Creator. The story goes that Abraham tried to convince his father of the error in worshiping idols, and one day, when left alone in his father's shop, he smashed every idol, with the exception of the largest one. When his father returned to find the idols destroyed, Abraham explained: "The idols got into a fight, and the big one smashed all the other ones." His father said, "Don't be ridiculous. These idols have no life or power. They can't do anything." To that Abraham replied, "Then why do you worship them?"

REFLECTION

Are there false "idols" in your life that act as "significance-blockers?" What are these external influences and what can you do to prune them from your path?

Christianity

As this chapter asks you to compare the beliefs and truths of world religions, consider this: Christianity began as a Jewish sect. The Bible contains the book of the "Tanakh," or Jewish scriptures. Many people who practice a certain religion are never aware their own faith contains so many similarities to another because they are too busy focusing on their differences.

Christianity, though one religion, is a collection of unique believers and different denominations: Catholics, Orthodox, Protestants, and others. All of these people, however, are united by prevailing beliefs and universal truths that lead them to pursue significance in a more fulfilling life for themselves and others.

Being the dominant religion in America, Christianity often becomes obscured behind piles of political and social baggage. However, it's a revolutionary belief system in its focus on empowering all men and women. Just as significance teaches that small acts which produce seismic changes in the life of even one person are the greatest acts of all, Jesus taught that the person who gives everything for his or her faith, such as the widow in the New Testament, is the most blessed.

Christianity is the only monotheistic faith which preaches that each person is a manifestation of God—not a servant, but a co-creator. That is significance. We all have the power to co-create the world around us each day, to shape it in new ways by giving blood, reaching out to the homeless, mentoring a child or countless other acts. When we change lives, we create a new world going forward from that moment.

Core Values

- Love God.
- Love your neighbor as yourself.
- Forgive.
- Reach the lost.
- Follow the teachings of Jesus as Savior.

Expression of a Universal Truth

The real security of Christianity is to be found in its benevolent morality, in its exquisite adaptation to the human heart, in the facility with which its scheme accommodates itself to the capacity of every human intellect, in the consolation which it bears to the house of mourning, in the light with which it brightens the great mystery of the grave.

—*Thomas B. Macaulay, nineteenth century British poet, historian, and politician*

Significance Icon

You expected to read about Jesus of Nazareth, right? Well, surprise. Jesus is, of course, at the heart of Christianity, but since He was a figure beyond mere mortal, He's not a great representation of the struggle for significance. John the Baptist was a forerunner of Jesus and a prophet who preached the importance of turning away from sin and being baptized. He grew up and prophesized from the wilderness, teaching people that escaping from sin and becoming baptized signified the drowning of their old life and their emergence from the water into a new life. When confronted or ridiculed about his devotion to Jesus, John had a great understanding of his role, seeing himself as a servant and explaining that he was merely the messenger sent to lay the path for something greater. In all his endeavors, John saw himself as the one serving, not the point of interest or the center of attention.

Islam

A deeply misunderstood religious tradition, Islam is actually a sibling faith to Judaism and Christianity, born from the family of Abraham, who is seen as the Father of the three great monotheistic religions. A deeply proud and intense faith that has sadly been tainted by perceptions of violence in recent years, Islam nonetheless continues to grow, buoyed in part by a stringent code of courtesy and respect and a powerful sense of justice.

Islam is actually a stern, humble, and rigorous faith built around Five Pillars:

1. *Shahadah*, faith in the Oneness of God and that Muhammad is His prophet.
2. *Salah*, the five daily prayers.
3. *Zakaat*, concern for and almsgiving to the needy.
4. *Sawm*, or fasting during the holy month of Ramadan.
5. The *Hajj*, the pilgrimage to Mecca for those who are able-bodied.

Core Values

- Love God.
- Show mercy and compassion.
- Love your neighbor.
- Give to charity.
- Affirm human dignity and pride.
- Treat guests and strangers with respect and humility.
- Be a voice for the voiceless.

Expression of a Universal Truth

The Islamic teachings have left great traditions for equitable and gentle dealings and behavior, and inspire people with nobility and tolerance. ... Islam is replete with gentleness, courtesy, and fraternity.

—*H.G. Wells, British writer, sociologist, and historian*

Significance Icon

It is said that the Prophet Muhammad, who was seen as the restorer of the original Islamic faith, could bring even his most dangerous enemies "to the fold of Islam" even without adequate funds or resources. Muhammad, through the influence of Islam, was able to unite idol worshipers, promoters of war, and abusers of human dignity. Despite persecution and exile, Muhammad and his followers continued to promote the virtues of Islam. By declaring righteousness as the only measurement of merit and honor, Islam allowed people an opportunity to reach new levels of spirituality and dignity. The rules of Islam spread through Muhammad were very basic and already in line with human nature, which made them easy to follow, allowing them to quickly shape people's cultural, moral, social, and spiritual lives.

> ***Significance Icon:*** *An individual who embodies the universal truths and philosophies of a given spiritual tradition.*

Hinduism

Hinduism is the world's third-largest religion, and the primary faith of India, where more than nine hundred million people practice it. It may be the world's oldest faith, going back to the Iron Age Vedic religion of India, and has many faces: one god, many gods, and some branches that believe in pantheism (God in everything) and reincarnation, the belief that after death each human returns to life in a new form according to his karma, his acts of justice or evil in the previous life.

Hinduism is deeply personal and there are many forms and aspects to its practice, including Vedantic, a deeply philosophical branch, and Yogic, which is based on the Yoga Sutras of Patanjali and is the source of what we think of as yoga today. At its core, Hinduism deals with a few core ideas: *dharma,* the essence of an individual's ethics and duties in life; *samsara,* the eternal cycle of birth, death, and rebirth; *karma,* which can be described as the principle of "as ye sow, so shall ye reap"; and *moksha,* liberation from the cycles of death and rebirth and ascension to a higher plane. Much of the faith's practices deal with opening the mind and consciousness to encourage us to see the divine in ourselves and daily life.

Core Values

- Ten duties = the Golden Rule.
- All people are one and should be treated with respect, kindness, justice, and compassion.
- Find meaning beyond self, possessions, and pleasure.
- Show kindness to all creatures.
- Flee immorality.

Expression of a Universal Truth

Hinduism is a relentless pursuit of Truth. "Truth is God" and if today it has become moribund, inactive, irresponsive to growth, it is because we are fatigued; and as soon as the fatigue is over, Hinduism will burst upon the world with a brilliance perhaps unknown before.

—Mohandas K. Gandhi, Indian political and spiritual leader

Significance Icon

If there is any figure who towers above all others in the Hindu tradition, it is Mohandas Gandhi, the Britain-educated lawyer who became an anti-violence freedom fighter for Indian independence. In his embrace of persistent yet passive protest, his transcendent belief in higher principles of justice and compassion, and his belief that any suffering can be endured if the cause is right, Gandhi was and remains a figure of light and enlightenment for millions.

Buddhism

Buddhism is not expressly a religion, as Buddhists do not believe in a Supreme Being. Instead, it would be more accurately described as a belief system, a set of ideals, codes, and philosophies intended to guide its followers to enlightenment, which is a complete loss of the sense of separation from the world. Some Buddhists believe in reincarnation, while others do not; most are atheists and instead view the divine as existing as an inherent part of the cosmos, as well as within man.

The peace-loving aspects of Buddhism have endeared it to many Westerners, but it is a faith of strict discipline. Buddhist monks are among the most disciplined meditators in the world, and have subjected themselves to many scientific studies on the effects of meditation on the brain. Buddhism can be seen as, in many ways, the epitome of the human path to surrendering the need for exterior success in order to become a wiser, stronger being without any need for self-gratification. It is a deeply humble and self-critical belief system—something welcome in this age of fundamentalism.

Core Values

- Sacrifice on behalf of the suffering people of the world.
- Wealth and comfort cannot provide meaning and purpose.
- Strive for simplicity, charity, and self-denial.
- Practice welfare and compassion for others.
- Rid the world of ignorance and suffering.
- Practice benevolence and aversion to injury of others.

Expression of a Universal Truth

My own Buddhist upbringing has helped me more than anything else to realize and to express in my speeches and writings this concept of world citizenship. As a Buddhist, I was trained to be tolerant of everything except intolerance. I was brought up not only to develop the spirit of tolerance, but also to cherish moral and spiritual qualities, especially modesty, humanity, compassion, and, most important, to attain a certain degree of emotional equilibrium.

—U Thant, Burmese diplomat and third Secretary-General of the United Nations

Significance Icon

Siddhartha Gautama, the founder of Buddhism, was born in the city of Lumbini and was raised in Kapilavastu. According to the Tipitaka, he was born a prince. Shortly after his birth, a wise man visited his father, King Śuddhodana. The wise man said Siddhartha would either become a great king (chakravartin) or a holy man (Sadhu), based on whether he saw life outside of the palace walls. Determined to make Siddhartha a king, Śuddhodana shielded his son from the unpleasant realities of daily life and sought to indulge him with a life of luxury. Even though his father provided him with everything he could ever want or need, Siddhartha always felt that accumulating material wealth was not the ultimate purpose in life.

At the age of twenty-nine, Siddhartha ventured outside the palace complex several times, despite his father's wishes. As a result, he discovered the suffering of his people, through encounters with an old man, a diseased man, a decaying corpse, and an ascetic. These are known among Buddhists as The Four Sights, one of the first contemplations of Siddhartha.

Eventually, The Four Sights prompted Siddhartha to be free from suffering by living the life of a mendicant ascetic, a highly respected spiritual practice at the time in ancient India. He left the palace, abandoning royal life to take up his spiritual quest, eventually finding companions with similar spiritual goals. Legend holds that he sat beneath a bodhi tree contemplating the nature of existence, until the realization that it was attachment—to material possessions, to other people, even to one's own life—that were the cause of all suffering. He became the Buddha, or one who attains perfect enlightenment or nirvana.

After years of practicing an ascetic life under numerous teachers and trying to find enlightenment through self-deprivation that nearly led to his death, Siddhartha discovered what some Buddhists call the "Middle Way," or a life of moderation. For the rest of his enlightened life, Siddhartha is said to have traveled the land teaching his spiritual doctrines to people of all walks of life, rich and poor, old and young, innocent or previously depraved. Among Buddhists, he is generally recognized as the Supreme Buddha of our age.

Confucianism

Confucianism is not so much a religious faith as a philosophical system for living and regarding the world. It is a complex system of moral, social, political, philosophical, and semi-religious thinking that has powerfully influenced the culture and history of Asia. The system Confucius taught was not about God or afterlife but a code of living based on morality, virtue, ethics, justice, common wisdom, and right action.

The great sage and philosopher believed, for example, that in a wise society, leaders should be chosen based on their wisdom, justice, ability, and ethics, rather than on social status, wealth, or the ability to lead armies. In our age of corruption and moral ambiguity in our leaders, this would certainly seem to be a philosophy whose time has come again.

Core Values

- Wisdom is rooted in deep love and respect for others.
- Jen = goodness, virtue, charity, or love.
- Focus on humanity in five areas: government, parental, conjugal, fraternal, and friendship.

Expressions of a Universal Truth

We shall, in fact, dig the grave of Western civilization unless we implement the faith that Confucianism and democracy have in common, namely, that ethics has its roots in man's relation to the universe, that morality comes into being through honest, clear-cut human relationships and cannot endure unless it is reflected in the patterns of daily life.

—Agnes E. Meyer, journalist, community activist, and philanthropist

The superior man has nine wishes. In seeing, he wishes to see clearly. In hearing, he wishes to hear distinctly. In his expression, he wishes to be warm. In his appearance, he wishes to be respectful. In his speech, he wishes to be sincere. In handling affairs, he wishes to be serious. When in doubt, he wishes to ask. When he is angry, he wishes to think of the resultant difficulties. And when he sees an opportunity for gain, he wishes to think of righteousness.
—*Confucius, Chinese philosopher*

Significance Icon

The philosophy of Confucianism was spread by the Chinese intellectual and philosopher Confucius (551-479 BC), who was widely admired for his values of personal morality, sincerity, correctness, and justice. Brought up in poverty, Confucius grew to be part of the "shi" class, which was known for the will of its people to seek social status based on talent and skill, rather than lineage or wealth. In his teaching, Confucius put the greatest emphasis on study and learning, causing many of his followers to call him the "Greatest Master." His message was that people needed to think for themselves and be conscious of the world around them, the experiences of the common person, and the moral issues present in their social and political worlds.

Struggling to spread his beliefs during a time of division and war, Confucius believed that if rulers were chosen according to morals and virtues, the "world" could be unified. His practice of "virtue ethics" promoted self-cultivation, empathy, and skilled judgment, as opposed to the imposition of rules and regulations.

With much of his teachings surrounding the concept of "righteousness," Confucius taught that, while self-interest isn't always bad, one could be a better, more honorable person if life was based on making decisions designed to promote society or the greater good.

Significance Exercise #8: Your Faith Tradition

Most people have some sort of spiritual tradition or belief, whether it's based on an organized religion or a more general spirituality. In any case, this faith shapes our search for significance. How does your faith affect your evolution and your progress toward significance?

Answer each faith-related question as completely as possible.

1. What kind of religion or spirituality do you subscribe to?

2. What do you consider to be its core teachings?

3. How have you modified those teachings to fit your universal truths and moral code?

4. How does your spiritual path shape your pursuit of significance (i.e., directing you to charity and helping others)?

5. How would your search for significance differ if you were not part of this spiritual tradition?

Stretching for Significance and Finding Common Ground

I recently traveled to Dubai on assignment for Florida's Blood Centers and was engaged in a very spirited discussion with one of my hosts. I am Christian and he is Muslim. If you only considered common ideas and beliefs about the differences between those two religions or our respective backgrounds, you might assume we had trouble in our discussion. The reality is we both were engaged in problem solving because we first linked our core beliefs to understand how we could meet the needs of our fellow human beings. Despite our differences, we were about helping others first. His comment that I will always treasure was this: "Islamic, Christian, and Jew must draw upon the common beliefs and our God to reach out and do good work together in His name."

True to this statement, each of the religions reviewed in this chapter shared some common traits. All too often, we focus on ourselves—or our differences with others—as we strive to "succeed." Instead, our goal should be to seek significance by acknowledging our common ground.

But your connection to a more significant life does not have to depend on your association with a religion. This chapter was meant to show that when we relate to and rally around the common value of bettering ourselves for the good of each other, great things can be done, regardless of our backgrounds or beliefs. Significance on behalf of furthering the human condition and bettering our world is something all enlightened beings, whatever name they attach to their beliefs, share. If you are well on your way to becoming significant, you share the same birthright and bear these values at the core of your being:

- Love for others
- Service of others
- Sharing of wealth with the needy
- Treating others with respect
- Building family
- Respect for life
- Protection for the weak
- Pursuit of peace and justice

> ### *REFLECTION*
>
> It's easy to spot differences. They are obvious: tall, short, fat, skinny, funny, somber, etc. A significant life is one that seeks similarities to forge partnerships that can lead to a greater good. In any group, we naturally gravitate to those people most like us. It is true that having a common link can make relationships easier, but a significant life doesn't settle for easy. Begin your search for significance by searching for similarities with people you may not think share much in common with you.

A New Universal Truth

This chapter has been about universal truths, and it is time for a new one based on significance. Since so much of what I write about regards leaders and their choices in favor of success or significance, this new universal truth will apply to CEOs and leaders as well:

> *It is time to rediscover honor, ethics, and morals in the development of our leaders, and to make these qualities as central to their training as finance or business strategy. If society is to evolve in the direction of significance, we must usher in a paradigm shift: a redefinition of what it means to be successful.*

This will not be easy. Shattering an old paradigm never is. Yet I believe this can be done, and it must be done. It isn't enough to penalize and arrest and condemn; that's letting significancer grow and then killing the patient with chemotherapy. How much better to prevent it by teaching honor, right action, and significance to our young leaders—then rewarding them not just for increasing year-to-year profits but for doing good? That is an ultimate truth we can all believe in.

Next Steps for Significance Seekers...

- *... Attend a service or meeting of each of the spiritual traditions in this book.*

- *... How are they alike?*

- *... How do they differ?*

- *... Which surprised you the most?*

- *... If you could create your own religious faith tradition from scratch, what would it be? What would it stand for? What would its objectives be?*

CHAPTER FIVE
Are You Significant?

A SELF-TEST THAT HELPS DETERMINE YOUR SIGNIFICANCE QUOTIENT, OR SQ

What do we mean by setting a man free? You cannot free a man who dwells in a desert and is an unfeeling brute. There is no liberty except the liberty of some one making his way towards something. Such a man can be set free if you will teach him the meaning of thirst, and how to trace a path to a well. Only then will he embark upon a course of action that will not be without significance.

—Antoine de Saint-Exupery, French pilot and author of The Little Prince

I've given you examples and presented you with abstract concepts, but now it's time to apply the concept of significance in a practical, personal way. It's time to find out how significant you are today, right now. We've all been in a social situation of some kind or another—in school, at a new job, at a party, or at a networking event. Imagine you go to a party and you and have conversations with ten people you've never met. If three days after the party someone were to ask those ten people what they thought of you, what do you think their response would be?

Part of significance is rooted in being a person of impact, leaving an impression, or inspiring each person with whom you come into contact. As a person seeking significance, your desire is not to be evaluated by your appearance or how you measure up to someone's expectations; your hope should be to leave an impression through the things you say and your actions.

People should remember you because your encounter with them was one they remember as being genuine and meaningful.

Another way to gauge your own significance is through self-reflection. Because this can be an abstract exercise, this chapter contains a rigorous examination that will help you determine your "SQ," or "Significance Quotient."

> **Significance Quotient:** *A scale of seventy to three-hundred fifty points that represents the current level of your evolution toward significance based on the Seven Pillars.*

The Test

The SQ Self-Test is in a simple format. It's divided into seven sections, one for each of the seven aspects of significant people. The idea is to assess how advanced you are in each of these seven vitally important qualities, so you know how you need to grow in the future to reach your own significance. For each statement, mark the appropriate number to rate yourself on a scale of one to five:

1—You disagree completely with the statement.
2—You disagree somewhat with the statement.
3—You're neutral on or unsure about the statement.
4—You agree somewhat with the statement.
5—You agree completely with the statement.

At end of the test, you'll find out what your total score means. So please go through each section and try to be as honest and introspective as you can. Remember, the more open you are, even to uncomfortable truths, the more you will benefit.

The Significance Quotient Self-Test

1. Discernment

Are you able to see the truth of others while having a clear perception of your own strengths and weaknesses? Do you have the ability to be honest with yourself about your shortcomings while honoring the qualities that are assets in your quest for significance? These questions will highlight your ability to perceive your own character and that of others.

1. I regard times of crisis as times I can learn about myself.
   Completely Disagree   1   2   3   4   5   Completely Agree

2. I am usually able to recognize when people are being truthful about their motives.
   Completely Disagree   1   2   3   4   5   Completely Agree

3. I am fully aware of my greatest flaws.
   Completely Disagree   1   2   3   4   5   Completely Agree

4. I judge others not by their position or title but by how their actions match their words.
   Completely Disagree   1   2   3   4   5   Completely Agree

5. I try to associate with those who are as fully self-realized as possible.
   Completely Disagree   1   2   3   4   5   Completely Agree

6. I don't compare my achievements to those of others.
   Completely Disagree   1   2   3   4   5   Completely Agree

7. I have distinct goals for the next five, ten, and twenty years.
   Completely Disagree   1   2   3   4   5   Completely Agree

8. I am my own harshest critic.
   Completely Disagree   1   2   3   4   5   Completely Agree

9. Some of the most trying times of my life have proved to be the most valuable.
   Completely Disagree   1   2   3   4   5   Completely Agree

10. I am very good at accepting criticism from others.
    Completely Disagree   1   2   3   4   5   Completely Agree

TOTAL SCORE FOR THIS SECTION: _____

2. Activism

Activists don't sit back and complain when things go wrong; as the name suggests, they take action. If you're not comfortable sitting on the sidelines but instead consider yourself a problem-solver and a teacher, then you have a strong activist strain in you.

11. When things go wrong, my first instinct is to pitch in and help fix them.
    Completely Disagree   1   2   3   4   5   Completely Agree

12. I am a natural entrepreneur.
    Completely Disagree   1   2   3   4   5   Completely Agree

13. People tend to turn to me for ideas when plans don't work out, assuming I will be able to come up with a solution.
    Completely Disagree   1   2   3   4   5   Completely Agree

14. Helping others gives me the greatest satisfaction I have ever experienced.
    Completely Disagree   1   2   3   4   5   Completely Agree

15. I get impatient with those who complain about the decisions of others instead of taking decisive action themselves.
    Completely Disagree   1   2   3   4   5   Completely Agree

16. I sit on the board of a nonprofit or am involved with a community, neighborhood, or activist organization.
    Completely Disagree   1   2   3   4   5   Completely Agree

17. I believe it's more important to provoke change than to be politically correct.
    Completely Disagree   1   2   3   4   5   Completely Agree

18. I enjoy being the "go to" person for my friends or colleagues.
    Completely Disagree   1   2   3   4   5   Completely Agree

19. I am naturally extremely organized and am always making plans.
    Completely Disagree   1   2   3   4   5   Completely Agree

20. At least once in the last five years I have spent my time or money to aid people whom I have never met.
    Completely Disagree   1   2   3   4   5   Completely Agree

TOTAL SCORE FOR THIS SECTION: _____

3. Reflection

Life seems to happen at one hundred miles per hour, and someone is always passing or tailgating. But living at high speed is a choice; so is reflection. People who live more in the moment, who take the time to appreciate life as it is happening, and who possess the self-perception to catch themselves when they begin to sprint with the rest of the rats, are rare indeed.

21. I often take time to stop what I'm doing and savor the moment.
    Completely Disagree   1   2   3   4   5   Completely Agree

22. I make a deliberate effort to meet and talk with new people wherever I am.
    Completely Disagree   1   2   3   4   5   Completely Agree

23. I have maintained or currently maintain a journal.
    Completely Disagree   1   2   3   4   5   Completely Agree

24. At day's end, I sit back during a quiet moment and think about everything that happened and what I learned.
    Completely Disagree   1   2   3   4   5   Completely Agree

25. I am blessed and wealthy in the ways that matter most.
    Completely Disagree   1   2   3   4   5   Completely Agree

26. Even if I don't always succeed, I try hard to make time for the pursuits that lend my life joy, meaning, and richness.
    Completely Disagree   1   2   3   4   5   Completely Agree

27. I have a strong spiritual side, whether I subscribe to a traditional religion or not.
    Completely Disagree   1   2   3   4   5   Completely Agree

28. I have a mental library of great authors, thinkers, and mentors upon whose wisdom I rely constantly.
    Completely Disagree   1   2   3   4   5   Completely Agree

29. I believe the statement that "The unexamined life is not worth living."
    Completely Disagree   1   2   3   4   5   Completely Agree

30. I don't fear mistakes; they are my best opportunity to learn and grow.
    Completely Disagree   1   2   3   4   5   Completely Agree

TOTAL SCORE FOR THIS SECTION: _____

4. Self-Esteem

Self-love is the cornerstone of everything; you can't love others if you don't love yourself. Significant individuals carry with them a strong foundation of self-respect and are willing to fight for the things in life that they know they deserve. Being significant means balancing humility with the willingness to take care of your own needs so you can be a beacon to others.

31. I love who I am today and who I am becoming.
    Completely Disagree   1   2   3   4   5   Completely Agree

32. I know when to practice "enlightened selfishness" and go after the things in life that I know I have a right to, such as respect from others, fair treatment, and earned rewards.
    Completely Disagree   1   2   3   4   5   Completely Agree

33. I am not shy about taking credit when my performance exceeds my expectations.
    Completely Disagree   1   2   3   4   5   Completely Agree

34. When I fall short, I don't beat myself up; instead, I vow to learn and do better next time.
    Completely Disagree   1   2   3   4   5   Completely Agree

35. I feel free to be completely myself with others, quirks and all, confident that they will respect and appreciate me.
    Completely Disagree   1   2   3   4   5   Completely Agree

36. If I am feeling undervalued, I take immediate action to rectify the situation.
    Completely Disagree   1   2   3   4   5   Completely Agree

37. I never tolerate disrespect or abuse in my personal relationships.
    Completely Disagree   1   2   3   4   5   Completely Agree

38. I deserve the best from every aspect of my life.
    Completely Disagree   1   2   3   4   5   Completely Agree

39. I work hard to keep my body and mind fit and healthy.
    Completely Disagree   1   2   3   4   5   Completely Agree

40. I don't let the drama or troubles of others get me depressed; I stay centered so I can be of help to them.
    Completely Disagree   1   2   3   4   5   Completely Agree

TOTAL SCORE FOR THIS SECTION: _____

5. Principles

The old saying "If you don't stand for something, then you'll fall for anything" applies to people of significance. Perhaps more than any of the Seven Keys, principles are the most obvious marker of a significant person. Significant individuals live by a tightly woven fabric of essential codes and moral precepts that guide their every decision.

41. I believe in the concept of honor and think it's perfectly relevant in today's world.
    Completely Disagree   1   2   3   4   5   Completely Agree

42. There are some things I absolutely will never, ever do.
    Completely Disagree   1   2   3   4   5   Completely Agree

43. In letting my morals and ethics guide me, I think of a beloved parent, grandparent, or other mentor and how I wish to make that person proud of me.
    Completely Disagree   1   2   3   4   5   Completely Agree

44. If possible, I always keep my word, no matter what the cost or inconvenience.
    Completely Disagree   1   2   3   4   5   Completely Agree

45. Some things are always right or always wrong, no matter what the culture or circumstances.
    Completely Disagree   1   2   3   4   5   Completely Agree

46. Someone who cannot keep a promise could never work for me.
    Completely Disagree   1   2   3   4   5   Completely Agree

47. I have a holy book or spiritual tradition that guides my personal code of right and wrong.
    Completely Disagree   1   2   3   4   5   Completely Agree

48. I would give up a financial reward or pass on an opportunity if it meant compromising my values … even if no one else would know.
    Completely Disagree   1   2   3   4   5   Completely Agree

49. I would decline to do business with someone whose actions or reputation violated my sense of ethics or morals.
    Completely Disagree   1   2   3   4   5   Completely Agree

50. I still recall a life lesson in morals or ethics even though it occurred many years or decades ago.
    Completely Disagree   1   2   3   4   5   Completely Agree

TOTAL SCORE FOR THIS SECTION: _____

6. Humility

James Barrie, the creator of *Peter Pan*, said, "The praise that comes from love does not make us vain, but more humble." That is true. True humility does not mean turning the other cheek or refusing to take credit for your work, but having the perspective to know you are just one piece in a marvelous machine of humanity. The humble, significant person remains quiet about his or her accomplishments, knowing there are always things that are greater and people who have done more with less.

51. I don't need public approval or credit to feel good about the things I do to help others.
    Completely Disagree   1   2   3   4   5   Completely Agree

52. I love it when other people get center stage for their accomplishments, even if that takes the spotlight off of me.
    Completely Disagree   1   2   3   4   5   Completely Agree

53. I don't boast. I let my actions speak for themselves.
    Completely Disagree   1   2   3   4   5   Completely Agree

54. Only people who lack confidence need to be boastful.
    Completely Disagree   1   2   3   4   5   Completely Agree

55. I don't have a problem admitting I don't know something.
    Completely Disagree   1   2   3   4   5   Completely Agree

56. I always give my full attention to others when I speak with them.
    Completely Disagree   1   2   3   4   5   Completely Agree

57. I am able to laugh at myself and do so quite often.
    Completely Disagree   1   2   3   4   5   Completely Agree

58. A person's achievements should be judged on what he or she had to overcome or sacrifice to achieve them and not just on the achievements themselves.
    Completely Disagree   1   2   3   4   5   Completely Agree

59. Small things—children, sunsets, music—are constant reminders to keep what I have done in perspective.
    Completely Disagree   1   2   3   4   5   Completely Agree

60. I never fail to give credit to others—family, mentors, colleagues—when I speak about my actions.
    Completely Disagree   1   2   3   4   5   Completely Agree

TOTAL SCORE FOR THIS SECTION: _____

7. Mindfulness

Mindful individuals do not live on autopilot. They relish the moments of love, peace, beauty, and courage that come along much more often than we realize. They cherish the people with whom they work, and as a result, inspire them.

61. Every moment of every day is a gift.
    Completely Disagree   1   2   3   4   5   Completely Agree

62. I take time each day to meditate, pray, reflect, or otherwise let my mind rest and commune with something higher.
    Completely Disagree   1   2   3   4   5   Completely Agree

63. I don't take the people I work with for granted; I try always to make sure they know how much I appreciate them.
    Completely Disagree   1   2   3   4   5   Completely Agree

64. I try often to see situations or problems from a novel angle in order to find a solution.
    Completely Disagree   1   2   3   4   5   Completely Agree

65. I am not a person who tends to follow peer pressure or conventional wisdom.
    Completely Disagree   1   2   3   4   5   Completely Agree

66. I think things happen for a reason.
    Completely Disagree   1   2   3   4   5   Completely Agree

67. I have a strong sense of purpose in my life and am always working to discover and/or further that purpose.
    Completely Disagree   1   2   3   4   5   Completely Agree

68. I am aware of my own mortality and have come to terms with it.
    Completely Disagree   1   2   3   4   5   Completely Agree

69. I think about my legacy.
    Completely Disagree   1   2   3   4   5   Completely Agree

70. I keep other people "grounded."
    Completely Disagree   1   2   3   4   5   Completely Agree

TOTAL SCORE FOR THIS SECTION: _____

YOUR TOTAL SIGNIFICANCE QUOTIENT: _____

You Did It!

If you answered each question openly and courageously, then you found some of them difficult. You were forced to do some soul searching and reject the easy answer. Good. We all have growing to do; no one is perfectly evolved or perfectly significant. That's all right. Part of the joy of living and becoming significant is knowing that no matter what heights you reach, you can always find new ways to challenge yourself and reach just a little higher, love a little stronger.

The first time I took this quiz, I surprised myself with some of my responses. I could have asked a hundred more questions about these topics; it's a subject that's endlessly fascinating. But then we would have a quiz too long to finish. These seventy questions should give you a great deal of insight into where you are today on your journey to significance. Just as important, they will make you think; you may never have even thought about some of these issues before. That's good. I want to shake you up with this book and ensure you're never complacent on life's path. This self-test is a wonderful step in that direction.

But now, to the scoring. First, there are no right or wrong answers. There's just you. You are not finished living or growing or learning, so any score is not a judgment. It's a progress report. It's a baseline of your emotional, spiritual, and intellectual development. It's a starting point and identifies aspects of yourself that need some work. So let's score it.

The best answer for each question is a five, meaning "Completely Agree." So each set of ten questions has a perfect total of fifty points. How close you are in each of the seven sections to that perfect score tells you how high your Significance Quotient is for that key. Add the scores together and you know your overall SQ. That tells you where you stand, overall, in becoming a more significant human being. Write down your scores for each section and rate them based on this scale:

41-50 in a section:

This is one of your strengths. You are highly evolved in this area and should consider it one of the foundational aspects of your character. Doubtless, other people see that, too. Well done.

31-40 in a section:

Not bad. You need a little bit of work, but you're above average in this area. There are some areas to work on, but you are probably already aware of them and making plans to address them. That's great—self-discovery and change are what this book is about.

21-30 in a section:

You're in the average range in this area, not particularly enlightened but not self-sabotaging, either. You have a great deal of room for improvement, and with this book you have the means of making that improvement part of your life.

20 or below in a section:

You have a great deal of work to do, because in this area you're not just treading water but slowly sinking. This characteristic is dragging you down and holding you back, so it's vital that you start making changes soon, as it's easier to break bad habits earlier in life rather than later.

Overall Significance Quotient Ratings

Add your seven scores together to get your SQ, keeping in mind that it's nothing more than a snapshot of where you are today. Where you are in a year or ten years is entirely up to you. I, for one, believe you have what it takes to be a significance genius. If you didn't, you wouldn't be investing your time reading this book.

SQ	Name	Meaning
321-350	Significance Genius	You're already a highly significant human being. Your highest purpose may be inspiring others to rise to your level.
276-320	Significance Prodigy	You're making excellent progress on your journey to significance, though you haven't reached all your goals yet.
226-275	Significance Seeker	You're part of the largest cohort in history: the body of humankind that is looking for meaning and purpose. It's a worthy search, and your goals are not out of reach.
150-225	Significance Student	As the name suggests, you have a great deal to learn and a long way to travel. Remain focused on your goal and remember that finding mentors and advisors along the way can help make a long road a bit shorter.
Below 150	Significance Enigma	You are at risk for living a life subject to the expectations of others and the shallow pleasures that bring no peace or meaning in the end. I suggest you find a mentor immediately so you can begin your journey.

What is your Significance Quotient? Whatever it is, don't take it too seriously. Unless you plan to live from now to the end of your days without changing or growing, your SQ will grow and change, too. The question to ask is, what does your SQ mean? What actions should it compel you to take? What do you owe the people in your life who have helped you achieve a high SQ? What must you change to elevate a low SQ? Those are not easy questions. Fortunately, we're going to talk about some answers right now.

Next Steps for Significance Seekers...

- *... Give this quiz to three people who are at your same level of professional success.*

- *... Give it to three people who are at different levels of professional achievement.*

- *... Compare the results of both sets of tests. Do you see correlations between professional position and significance?*

- *... Come up with seven other key qualities you feel significant people have and create your own test (it doesn't have to be as long as this one).*

- *... For each of the Seven Pillars, how do you think you got to the point where you are today? What key milestones shaped those seven qualities in you?*

PART TWO:
BEING SIGNIFICANT

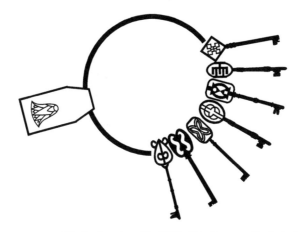

CHAPTER SIX

Seven Keys to Unlocking Your Significance

**CRUCIAL SPIRITUAL AND DEVELOPMENTAL STEPS
TO UNLOCK THE ESSENCE OF YOUR BEING**

If you wish to achieve worthwhile things in your personal and career life, you must become a worthwhile person in your own self-development.

—Brian Tracy, bestselling self-help author

Significance is not a state but a process, a dynamic act of self-evolution. That is one of the factors that make it so unlike the pursuit of success. When you are primarily concerned about reaching a certain income level or position within your field, you can reach a point where you are at the "finish line," whether that is the corner office and the title of CEO, a million-dollar annual income or some other metric. But when your life is built around acts and thoughts of creation, compassion, healing, and enrichment of others, you never reach a stopping point. Unlike economic growth, personal growth has no limits. When a truly significant individual achieves one goal, ten others open up; it's a natural part of the mindset.

No matter what you scored on the self-test—no matter what your Significance Quotient—you probably have room for improvement. Most of us are seeking information to guide our self-directed process of evolution, but it's hard to come by. How do you ask someone, "What should I do to become more significant?" Every individual has a unique "significance fingerprint," the qualities that make your life one of significance and not just empty material success. But there are seven key characteristics common to almost every person who has achieved a significant presence in this world. Mix them together in any way, augmenting your existing strengths and shoring up your weaknesses, and you get a recipe for astonishing personal development and self-renewal.

In the way the Seven Pillars show you where you are today in terms of being significant, the Seven Keys to significance define the road you must travel. They represent the highest qualities of the significant individual. Let's take a look at the Seven Keys—what they are, what they mean, and how they will affect the trajectory of your personal journey.

> **Significance fingerprint:** *The unique aspects of your life—charity work, pursuit of your passion, creating solutions that bring hope—that make you significant.*

1. Unconditional Love

It is virtually impossible to attain any measure of significance in your life without recognizing and appreciating the intrinsic value of the lives around you—without loving all the people you encounter, without judgment. As Americans, we live in a nation of excess. However, this is one area where our cupboards are bare. In order to find significance within, we must view others as significant and seek ways to help them on their journey.

When we say the word *love*, romantic gazes and walks in the moonlight come to mind. But the love that is needed on a journey toward significance is different. It is known as unconditional or *agape* love. The Greek word agape is defined as "love for another above self." This concept seems foreign in our culture. We are told it's all about us. Anything that boosts our self-esteem is okay, even if that esteem isn't earned. We're encouraged to be self-absorbed. None of these messages supports an agape mentality. Agape love cares for the unlovable and the unfamiliar, the faces you see every day and faces you will never know. When true agape love is a core belief in your system, judgmental and prejudicial attitudes cease. Agape love views the big picture, where lives are intertwined and the absence of one, no matter how insignificant it may seem, affects the whole.

Mother Teresa is a person who operated from pure agape love. She found significance in a life of poverty and fulfillment in actions motivated by her love for those she defined as "the hungry, the naked, the homeless, the crippled, the blind, the lepers, all those people who feel unwanted, unloved, uncared for throughout society, people that have become a burden to the society and are shunned by everyone." Unlike many in modern society, she saw every person as someone of worth, and she sacrificed herself to further enhance the lives of those people. Mother Teresa established her Missionaries of Charity in 1952. The twelve nuns working with her grew to thousands and spread into four-hundred fifty centers around the world. Her ministry grew not because of her strategic planning smarts, but because others were drawn to her complete dedication and desire to do the right thing. Her mission was one of service beyond self, undiluted agape love.

> **Agape love:** *Complete, enveloping love for another human spirit without judgment or need for reciprocation.*

The mother of a daughter with Down syndrome learned a lesson in unconditional love in a special way. Lisa loved to go with her mom to the local grocery store each week. Mr. Jones owned the establishment, which had been in his family for two generations. He was a tall, stately man with a gruff demeanor. The mother would have loved to shop at another store, but Lisa enjoyed going there. The employees knew her, loved her, and greeted her like royalty when they walked in. Lisa would quickly run to each of her friends, giving hugs and asking, "Where is Mr. Jones? Where is Mr. Jones?" Mr. Jones was always standing to the side of the entrance, glaring at Lisa's mother for the distracting effect her daughter had on his business. As soon as Lisa saw Mr. Jones, the reaction was always the same. She squealed his name and ran toward him as fast as her legs would carry. "I love you, Mr. Jones. I missed you so much. You are my favorite!" Lisa's outstretched arms met his cold embrace; it was clear he was tolerating her antics because her mother brought him business each week. After all of this, Lisa's mother would quietly bid him a good day as they went on with their shopping.

One day Lisa's mother decided to change things. "Honey, before we go to the store today, I want to talk with you about something," she said. "Mr. Jones doesn't seem to like hugs too much. Why don't you just give your other friends their hugs, but let's just leave Mr. Jones alone, OK?"

Lisa had already started laughing before her mother finished her request. "Mom, Mom, no, no, no. Mr. Jones *needs* my hugs. I see his heart smile when I hug him. I know he loves me. His heart smiles!" Lisa's mother braced herself for Mr. Jones' scorn as they made their way to the store. But when they arrived she saw a sign on the door: "MRS. KENDRICK—PLEASE BRING LISA TO MERCY HOSPITAL ROOM 356."

The ride to the hospital was anxious. Lisa was nervous and questioning over and over, "What's wrong, Mom?" When they arrived at the third floor, a nurse saw them coming off the elevator. "You must be Lisa."

Lisa looked at her and begged, "Do you have my Mr. Jones? He needs me."

"I believe you are right, Lisa," the nurse confirmed. She led them to the room where the once tall and stately Mr. Jones lay vulnerable in a hospital bed. He was covered with tubes and monitors, and the sounds hurt Lisa's ears. She approached the bed to see if it was really her friend.

"Mr. Jones?"

A squeal broke out as Lisa realized it was her Mr. Jones. She maneuvered her way around the medical equipment to throw her arms over his chest, trying to give him his hug. For the first time, Lisa's mother saw the gruff man smile.

"I love you, Mr. Jones. I missed you," Lisa exclaimed. But Mr. Jones finished the line.

"You're *my* favorite."

Lisa looked straight in the eyes of the man whose embrace had previously been so cold. With tears in her eyes, she asked to be sure she heard correctly.

"I'm *your* favorite?"

"Lisa, when I had this heart attack, all I could think about was I wished I had a hug from you. I'm sorry I never hugged you back before."

"That's OK, Mr. Jones. Your arms didn't know my hugs made your heart smile!"

Unconditional love breaks down barriers. A gruff old man realized how much that unconditional love meant when thought he might not have a chance to reciprocate.

Is there a "Mr. Jones" in your life? Someone who seems bitter and cold? Try Lisa's method. Look at the reaction that could be going on in the heart of this person. You never know if your pure love and approval might be the fire that keeps someone going.

What if we learned and practiced showing this kind of unconditional love to everyone in our workplaces, on the street, and in our homes? Little by little, such actions would become easier. Eventually they would become a habit that is understood, expected, and passed to generations that follow. We see this in Florida's Blood Centers all the time. People who are gallon or multi-gallon donors eventually bring their children in once they are old enough to become donors. It is a moving experience to see a simple act of service—agape love being passed down the family line to make an impact for lives today and generations to follow.

What kind of agape love gesture can you make today?

Significance Story

You may or may not have heard the term "The Beloved Community." But you will certainly recognize the name of the man who popularized and gave meaning to the term as it is known today: Dr. Martin Luther King Jr.

First used in the early twentieth century by philosopher Josiah Royce, the concept of The Beloved Community was adopted by King, who used it to refer to a global vision of when all people in the world could share in the wealth of the earth. To some, the phrase was just a lofty goal, an idyllic image of a world in which no problem or conflict exists. To King, however, The Beloved Community was a realistic and attainable objective that could be achieved if all people, in all places, committed to the principles and practice of nonviolence.

Recognizing that conflict was an unavoidable ingredient in the human experience, King did not avoid controversial issues. He merely believed all conflicts could be resolved peacefully if everyone involved committed to a nonviolent solution. King avoided referring to people in conflict as "enemies" or "opponents," and instead called them "adversaries." In The Beloved Community, he believed, adversaries could work things out together in a spirit of friendship and goodwill. King was actually a fervent follower of another significant leader discussed in this book: Gandhi. He admired Gandhi's belief that one should befriend enemies, as King believed the convention of loathing one's opponents was actually immoral and void of respect and human compassion.

According to the King Center, a living memorial dedicated to advancing Dr. King's legacy, in The Beloved Community hunger and homelessness would not exist because the international ideologies of human decency would not allow it. Prejudice and discrimination would be replaced by an atmosphere of all-embracing brotherhood. Instead of military power, international disputes would be solved with peaceful discussion and resolution. Basically, in The Beloved Community, love and peace prevail, always.

In fact, one of the core concepts of what King saw necessary for this type of unity was unconditional love. King said, "Agape love does not begin by discriminating between worthy and unworthy people … it begins by loving others for their sakes [and] makes no distinction between a friend and enemy."

We can all use King's concept of The Beloved Community as a model for our interaction with others when it comes to our personal quests for significance.

2. Spontaneous Generosity

"It's not my job!" How often have we heard that from colleagues? On the journey to significance, these words should not be part of the vocabulary. There are many lessons learned and blessings bestowed when we do things that are not required or expected. Going above and beyond the call of duty sometimes takes us above and beyond our own greatest expectations. The simplest gestures can mean a great deal to the recipient of the "random act of kindness."

An exterminator went to an apartment building one hot summer day for his routine spraying. He found a woman and her daughter stranded in their apartment; the little girl was running a fever and they needed to get to their doctor, but their car had a dead battery. He tried to jump the battery to no avail. His small pickup truck was not big enough to carry the mother and daughter along with his son, who was riding along for the day. So the exterminator wished the young mother well and began his walk back to his truck—then he saw the face of his son. He realized what a teachable moment he had before him.

He went back to the apartment and asked the woman about her battery. It was recently purchased and still under warranty. She even had the receipt. He said, "Let me take that back and get a new battery. I'll bring the new one back and put it in." Gratefully, she gave him the receipt. He looked at it and his heart sank. Walmart. The exchange line at Walmart was infamous for being long and time-consuming, not what you want when you are trying to run a small business. He shrugged, promised to return as soon as he could, and drove off. As he and his son waited in a long line to exchange the battery, his son looked up and asked, "Dad, don't you have a lot more appointments today?"

"Yes, I do."

"Why are you spending so much time with this lady's battery? Couldn't somebody else help her?"

"Someone else probably could, but you and I have the privilege of helping today."

Eventually, the man got and installed the new battery, watched it turn the engine over, and sent mother and daughter on their way. The woman drove away in tears of gratitude. The lesson was invaluable to an impressionable young boy who saw his dad was a man willing to sacrifice to make a difference in someone's day.

The exterminator was probably not familiar with Albert Schweitzer, but he embodied the essence of Schweitzer's quote: "You must give some time to your fellow men. Even if it's a little thing, do something for others, something for which you get no pay but the privilege of doing it."

One definition of privilege describes it as "an advantage or source of pleasure granted to a person." How can giving time when you already don't have enough of it be a source of pleasure? It is the way we are wired. Remember Maslow's Hierarchy of Needs? The pinnacle of self-actualization is growth and living beyond yourself. We are endowed with a desire to make a difference, to lead a meaningful existence. When we seize the opportunities presented throughout the day, as small as they may seem, we receive pleasure … if we allow it. Those who look only at the missed deadline or the tardy appointment will never enjoy the pleasure of becoming significant. Shakespeare's Hamlet once said, "Nothing is either good or bad but that thinking makes it so." How we view a situation determines how we define it.

How many opportunities do we allow to pass by every day? How many chances do we turn down? Life is busy. Schedules are hectic. But significance calls us to a higher concept of time, one defined not by how many tasks we can pack into a given span, but how great an impact we have on the lives of others each day. Time well-spent becomes not about checking off items on a to-do list, but about making a lasting difference in the present or future of even one of our fellow travelers.

Once you have learned to seize those small opportunities to make a difference, you begin to ask questions. "How can I keep this feeling going? How can I make it last longer?" The answer: *Give more.* Find your passion and give yourself to it. Volunteer at a children's hospital or a nursing home. Take the time to help out at a recovery center. Whatever it is, do it quietly. Don't expect the same pleasure to come to you if you seek appreciation for the tasks.

When your life is oriented on giving selflessly and completely, you will find yourself conflicted at times. You will face unpopular choices, people who don't understand, and sometimes serious sacrifice in order to serve your significance. That is when you find out just how committed you really are. The Reverend Martin Niemoller (1892-1984), a Protestant pastor in post-World War II Germany, did not start out as an advocate for freedom. He initially supported Hitler and showed a great deal of promise for moving up in the Nazi regime. However, he quickly grew disillusioned, and was later arrested and incarcerated for his open opposition to Hitler. He berated himself for not doing more, and penned these famous words:

When the Nazis came for the communists,
I remained silent;
I was not a communist.

When they locked up the social democrats,
I remained silent;
I was not a social democrat.

> *When they came for the trade unionists,*
> *I did not speak out;*
> *I was not a trade unionist.*
>
> *When they came for me,*
> *There was no one left to speak out.*

We have come a long way from Hitler. But every day in every city in America, there is injustice and pain. A life pursuing significance is willing to stand for justice and change, willing to speak for those whom society has cast out, as Jesus did.

3. Appreciation of Quiet Solitude

You may be saying, "Anne, you're crazy if you think I can even begin this process of self-reflection and self-reinvention with all that's going on! Too many things and people are clamoring for my time." That's when it's essential you have the discipline to shut down, unplug, turn off and, as Timothy Leary said, drop out. Seek a quiet place and time where you and your thoughts can be alone, and be militant about protecting it.

A college professor I know has a visual depiction of the need to prioritize our time. He shares his "big rocks" analogy where he fills a jar with small pebbles representing the little things that fill our day. When he tries to add big rocks, which represent our priorities for the day, they do not fit. He then pours out the pebbles and places the big rocks in first, then adds the pebbles. All the pebbles fit in place around the big rocks. The lesson: You must set your main priorities in place first, before the endless distractions of the day shatter them. Solitude is one of those rocks. Without it, you cannot begin to know who you are enough to know where you are on your journey to significance. It may require waking in the morning before others arise. It may require an appointment in your Blackberry. Whatever it takes, make the time to be alone.

We have programmed so much into each minute of the day that sometimes we don't have a clue as to how we arrived at our destination. Taking a moment to find solitude each day is key to significance. If you permit yourself to spend time alone, taking a break from the usual noise and activity occurring around you, you can become truly mindful of your thoughts and the big "rocks" that are most important to you. Instead of letting every moment be consumed by the rush of events hurtling past you, honor yourself by allowing your mind the time to reflect and fulfill your own emotional requirements. After all, we cannot fill others if we do not first take time to fill ourselves.

Dr. Jon Kabat-Zinn, the founder of Center for Mindfulness in Medicine, Health Care, and Society, expresses the effect of a lack of mindful solitude when he says: "We tend to run through our moments to get to other moments. You could live decades of your life on autopilot, driving through your life, missing what's most important and most fundamental. Then you end up dying, realizing that you haven't been there for the living." Solitude is about acknowledging, respecting, and awakening your "sacred self," the voice of timeless wisdom that is always speaking to you from the depths of your being but which is often drowned out by the rush of life's obligations. Each of us has a wellspring of eternal knowing, peace, and healing within us, but it is only in silence and contemplation that we allow it to bubble to the surface of our reasoning minds and be heard. Why do you think great yogis, monks, and shamans spend many years in silent meditative practice? They are trying to discover the divinity *within*, not without. That is what solitude can help you do.

There is a multitude of ways to enjoy solitude and practice mindfulness. Many practice yoga, as its very purpose is concerned with freedom from both spiritual and physical disturbances. At its core, yoga is meant to teach and engage the practitioner in introspection. Through introspection, one observes and visualizes obstacles that must be overcome, and comes to know one's self and the hindrances that obstruct one from significance. These barriers can be anything from aversion or attachment to ignorance or egoism. But through introspection, we can come to anticipate and avoid our own impediments, establishing for ourselves a clearer mind with which to guide ourselves and our decisions.

> **Mindfulness:** *The ability to quiet the rush of thoughts in the mind so you can become fully aware of your thoughts, feelings, and motivations.*

One of the greatest examples of seeking solitude for focus was Jesus Christ. During His brief three-year ministry, crowds bombarded Him. His close inner circle of twelve apostles was seeking His guidance yet often missing His point. He had a specific mission in His life. It required strength that in His human form, He could not find on His own. His source of power was prayer. He prayed to God, who sent Him on this tremendous journey of significance to help strengthen Him to complete His mission. Scriptures tell us He often retreated from the crowds and even His own core support group to pray. His apostle tells how, while it was still dark, Jesus got up, left the house, and went off to a solitary place, where He prayed. Luke confirmed that Jesus often withdrew to lonely places and prayed.

People of significance are able to draw from an inner source of strength and calm in the most challenging circumstances to achieve great tasks. Todd Beamer is known as one of the heroes of Flight 93. The hijackers of 9/11 planned to use that plane as yet another missile on that destructive day in our nation's history. As Todd and his group of passengers decided to strategize and retake the cockpit, he tried to call his wife. The Verizon operator trying to connect the call ended up as the witness of his last act prior to his moment of ultimate significance. Amid great distress, unrelenting pressure, and fear, Todd asked the operator to join him in reciting the Lord's Prayer prior to his final comment that began the end of that flight: "Let's roll!" Hopefully, none of us will have to encounter such a devastating situation. However, the way we act and respond in the small nuances of day-to-day challenges foreshadows how we would handle a major crisis.

Prayer and meditation are powerful tools in your fight for significance. Most core beliefs are formed by the acknowledgment of a higher power. The way to connect with that power and further bring those core beliefs into focus is to spend time in quiet solitude. You achieve focus, direction, and inner peace.

Significance Exercise #9: The Solitude Test

We're a society built around doing; introspection isn't one of our strengths. But significance demands that you develop the ability to stand in silence and let your mind drift, rest, and contemplate itself. This exercise tests your ability to do that.

For three consecutive days, find fifteen minutes to retreat to a place of total solitude where there is nothing to distract your senses: no TV, work, conversation, or cell phone. Get comfortable and breathe deeply. Let your mind drift; do not dwell on thoughts as they appear, but let them evaporate. Write down what you experience below.

Day #1	Time spent in solitude:	Describe the progress of your thoughts:	How hard it was to keep from being distracted (1-10, 1 = easy, 10 = impossible):	What did you learn from the experience?
Day #2	Time spent in solitude:	Describe the progress of your thoughts:	How hard it was to keep from being distracted (1-10, 1 = easy, 10 = impossible):	What did you learn from the experience?
Day #3	Time spent in solitude:	Describe the progress of your thoughts:	How hard it was to keep from being distracted (1-10, 1 = easy, 10 = impossible):	What did you learn from the experience?

4. Passion

In his book *The Passion-Centered Professional*, coach and speaker Gary Zelesky writes, "Your passion for life determines your position in life." That is completely true. People who lead significant lives have a common quality: passion. It may be a passion for the arts, education, helping those in poverty, or any of a thousand other things. But people of significance always find a way to take their passion and use it to bring greater joy to themselves and those around them.

What would motivate a young woman trying to teach a little girl who bit her, kicked her, and had parents who refused to discipline her? Passion. Anne Sullivan came to teach the deaf, blind, and mute Helen Keller with little training, but a great deal of passion. She remembered what it was like to be thought unworthy of an education. She drew on her experiences of overcoming obstacles to instill hope and passion into a child whom society saw as hopeless. Through her passion she was able spark the desire to learn in the heart of a young girl who had no dreams. The amazing accomplishments of Helen Keller have inspired generations of people with disabilities, and the passionate teamwork of Anne Sullivan and Helen Keller showed the world that even a person without sight, hearing, or speech can communicate a message that inspires the world. Where would Helen Keller have been without the passionate pursuit of Anne Sullivan?

Passion is the yeast in a life's recipe for significance. It enables us to rise above our circumstances and fulfill a greater purpose than we would be without it. Anne Sullivan's significance allowed her to rise above poverty, grief, and physical struggles to become the one who opened Helen Keller's world and opened a society's eyes toward the possibility of a life of light amid darkness.

Sometimes we develop passion out of necessity. Prior to actor Michael J. Fox's diagnosis of Parkinson's disease, he probably never thought about advocacy for research into cures for devastating diseases. While it is safe to assume Fox would rather live his life without Parkinson's, he has chosen to use his devastating diagnosis to push him into significance rather than self-pity. This quote reflects his passionate pursuit for a cure:

> *"This is the true joy in life, the being used for a purpose recognized by yourself as a mighty one; the being thoroughly worn out before you are thrown on the scrap heap; the being a force of nature instead of a feverish selfish little clod of ailments and grievances complaining that the world will not devote itself to making you happy."*
> —*George Bernard Shaw, nineteenth century Irish playwright*

There is a big difference between happiness and joy. Shaw knew that true joy in life has nothing to do with avoiding bad circumstances or challenges and everything to do with setting aside your own ailments and grievances in order to be used for a purpose you recognize as a mighty one.

> **Passion:** *That which you hunger to do or achieve, regardless of financial reward, obstacles, or social disapproval. Music, art, and travel are common passions.*

Fox kept his diagnosis private for many years and tried to carry on despite the challenging circumstances. Staying on top of medication cycles, he was able to manage his career as a television sitcom star. Ironically, it was after he realized he could no longer keep his ailment secret that he achieved a level of significance. His passion intersected with his pride. He allowed his celebrity status to be used to launch a foundation and raise funds for a cure. Researchers had told him Parkinson's was one of the few neurological disorders for which the research was way ahead of the funding. The hope of a cure in his lifetime has fueled Fox's passion to become an advocate. He achieved success when he privately managed his disease and continued with his acting career. But significance came when he went public and morphed from just another movie star into an advocate and symbol of hope.

So many of us are born to privilege and circumstance with all the right tools at our disposal. Could it be that having too much given to us can cripple our passion? Does having to work hard for something ignite a fire inside that would otherwise not generate a spark? Does overcoming hardship give us a greater possibility of finding our significant passion? Possibly, but a better bet is to start out in life with the default position of "passion first, practicality second." Too often, well-meaning parents, confronted by a child's career interest in an area such as art, music, or writing, will tell the child to "have something to fall back on." Practicality trumps joy. But a wise father's advice should be: "Find what you love to do. Then, figure out a way to get paid for it."

An MSNBC study recently documented Baby Boomers who were seeking a second career after retirement. It found that many were trying to supplement an income, but also find a passion. Executives are trading the boardrooms for classrooms as they become teachers. Stay-at-home moms are venturing from empty nests into nursing schools. While it is a joy to see people find happiness in their profession late in life, how much more could be accomplished if we began to seek passion earlier?

Others have found significance by bringing their passion into their profession. When we approach our careers from the inside out, instead of the outside in, we let our values and beliefs take the lead, instead of letting the marketplace, money, or status dictate our pursuits. Attorneys have traded lucrative careers as trial lawyers to work for legal aid. Others have made their work significant just by the way they approach their jobs. A janitor working for NASA in the 1960s was asked what he was doing. His reply was simple: "Putting a man on the moon." That response and sense of purpose comes from seeing the big picture and knowing your role has significance.

We see this same attitude among employees at Florida's Blood Centers. All of our leaders and employees give each other the RED treatment: Respect, Equality, and Dignity. Whether they are on the front lines or behind the scenes, at a desk or interacting with donors, all of our employees are respected and appreciated for their passion for helping others. No matter what their title, these people know their true objective is "delivering the right blood to the right patient at the right time."

Significance Story

When we think of Gandhi, the image that comes to mind is of a truly inspired individual who was a natural-born leader of people and advocate for independence. While Gandhi was all of these things and more, it wasn't until he discovered his passion for truth and equality that he was able to make a difference.

It is often overlooked that before Gandhi experienced the injustice of the world and understood his capacity to create change, he actually faced many challenges and disappointments and experienced several unsuccessful attempts in other fields of work.

Before he developed the principles and passions that compelled him later in life, Gandhi was a mediocre student at best, barely graduating from high school. He made an attempt at studying medicine, but failed and was forced to quit. When he first entered the legal arena, Gandhi was unhappy training as a barrister and had limited success when first trying to establish a law practice. In addition, he was once turned down when trying to become a high school teacher.

It was not until Gandhi experienced social injustice firsthand in South Africa, where he was unfairly denied entry and thrown off trains, barred from hotels, and beaten because of his ethnicity, that he realized his passion for social activism, equality, and independence. This time was a turning point in his life, leading him to his involvement in politics and his peaceful stewardship of Indian independence.

Gandhi's experiences, setbacks, and shortcomings are a lesson to all of us about the power passion can have in helping us achieve great things and finding significance in our lives.

5. Learning and Mentoring

The fire flew in fantastic sparks as the young apprentice sat closely by the side of the master blacksmith. He wiped his hands on the heavy leather apron and began to take his turn to intricately mold a horseshoe for the blacksmith's customer. His hands shook somewhat as he held the heavy tools. Thoughts rushed through his mind as he recounted the careful instruction and visualized the blacksmith's technique. As the young boy gazed into the fire heating the steel, he caught a glimpse of his teacher's smile. He proceeded with confidence, knowing he had been taught well and the man he trusted to teach him his trade approved. It was a memory frozen in the young boy's mind. A generation passed and the young boy, now a master blacksmith, handed his tools to another pair of young hands that belonged to an apprentice eager to please his master and perfect his skills. The fire flew in fantastic sparks as the blacksmith now gave an approving smile to the next generation's master.

Times were simpler during the early days of our country. The foundations of American entrepreneurship and enterprise were based on master and student relationships. These were not simple training sessions. Apprentices often went to live with their master teachers. They built strong relationship bonds that extended beyond their trade skills. The masters invested time in the apprentices that was honored by commitment to the goals and pursuits of excellence.

Somewhere along the way to today's world, we lost this intimate art of passing down skills and character. Maybe it is due to a society that values white-collar corporate jobs over skilled labor. Maybe it is because of the desire for instant gratification that working just to learn is not a pursuit young people are willing to embark upon. Regardless, we must bring back the master/teacher concept to the mainstream.

> **Mentor:** *An older, experienced expert in a field who passes on wisdom and lessons about the field to someone less experienced and serves as an example of how to practice and live.*

To be sure, the concept is not lost. There are internships in which students are encouraged or required to participate in order to earn a college degree. But while internships are valuable, they do not always build the character that underlies true greatness. Too often, they are seen as another means to an end—a plum job offer—than as an opportunity to develop personally. For significance to become a broad-based part of our culture, both ends of the mentoring equation—mentors and those seeking experience and growth—must actively pursue and create mentoring and apprenticeship opportunities.

One of the most significant lives to grace the twentieth century was that of Dr. Martin Luther King Jr. His leadership during a tumultuous time in our nation's history lives on today, inspiring and fostering racial understanding, and he could be seen legitimately as the philosophical wellspring of the presidency of Barack Obama. King's commitment and eloquence led a nation to take action based on the moral and ethical beliefs he presented: equality, nonviolence, brotherhood, and justice. These core values were established long before he was a world leader and a figure of national influence.

As a young boy, King was blessed with parents who understood the atrocities of discrimination but encouraged their son to live beyond them. He sat in church pews and watched congregations respond to his father, who was a great preacher in his own right, and other gifted orators. He knew early on that communication was powerful. While he wanted to follow in those footsteps, he was also raised to think independently and make his own decisions. His aggressive study enabled him to enter Morehouse College in Atlanta at the age of fifteen. It was there that King met the man he would later call his intellectual and spiritual father, Dr. Benjamin E. Mays. Dr. Mays influenced King through his dynamic Tuesday chapel orations as president of Morehouse, as well as personal time he spent with the young student. The close bond they established remained throughout their lives.

Mays undoubtedly achieved success through his work in academia. But his significance came with his 1948 chapel address that introduced a young student named Martin Luther King Jr. to Gandhi's philosophy of nonviolence. As they say, the rest is history.

Ruth Simmons, the president of Brown University, also had her life transformed by mentors. As she relates in a revealing *U.S. News and World Report* article, she was lucky enough to have a series of teachers who challenged her—first at her segregated high school, then at the mostly black Dillard College, and then at Wellesley College, whose female president forever upended her concept of gender roles. Simmons went on to earn a Harvard PhD in Romance languages and become president of Smith College, something she says would not have happened had she not had mentors to push her to excel.

Is there a young person in your life for whom you are willing to be the difference maker? Or are you someone seeking a mentor? Either way, mentoring and being mentored enable both parties to give the gift of knowledge and of taking in that knowledge, and then passing it on to another generation of learners. The mentored inevitably become the mentors, standing in the shadows while those they have taught go on to great achievements. They may be in shadow, but they bask in the light of significance, shining on them as shapers of the destinies of others.

6. Moderation

A certain degree of physical harmony and comfort is necessary, but above a certain level it becomes a hindrance instead of a help. Therefore the ideal of creating an unlimited number of wants and satisfying them seems to be a delusion and a snare.

—Mohandas Gandhi, Indian political and spiritual leader

"I want that!" Parents across America cringe as their toddlers learn a phrase that becomes a mainstay in their vocabulary for years to come. Watching television commercials, seeing the toys of other children, and riding starry-eyed in a cart through a toy store starts the insatiable desire for "More!"

As parents in such a wealthy culture, most all of us have given in to the wonderful feeling of meeting the desires and wants of our children. It brings joy. There is a smile. Many children are appreciative and give hugs. But how long before that gratitude turns into entitlement? We criticize our youth for wanting so much, but how do they learn such greed? Generally, the apple doesn't fall far from the tree. We may immediately defend our actions as wanting to give more to our children. That is a noble pursuit. However, in some cases our giving tends to hold them back.

How many wildly successful and significant men and women have spoken of their humble backgrounds, upbringings in which they lacked many material comforts but never wanted for love, encouragement, or the understanding of the all-powerful nature of hard work. The Horatio Alger Distinguished American Awards, given every year to people who personify that "up by the bootstraps" perseverance and vision, are all about moderation, delayed gratification, and commitment to a long-term goal. This is why in the pursuit of significance, moderation must be practiced.

Moderation is a virtue encouraged and adhered to by some of the greatest scholars, humanitarians, and leaders of history. Benjamin Franklin included "moderation" among his thirteen virtues to live by, which he published in *Poor Richard's Almanack*. A quote by Aristotle says, "It is better to rise from life as from a banquet—neither thirsty nor drunken." Seneca, a Roman philosopher from the Silver Age of Latin literature, also said, "It is the sign of a great mind to dislike greatness, and prefer things in measure to things in excess." We would be wise to heed these great men.

> **Simplicity:** *Living with only the possessions, occupation, and habitation that you need to sustain physical safety and health, mental tranquility and acuity, and spiritual peace and harmony—and nothing else.*

Chuck Underwood is a "generationalist." He has spent much time researching the behavior and attitudes of people based on their generational status: Silent, Baby Boomer, Generation X, Generation Y, and Millennial. One of his overviews demonstrates the drive of the Baby Boomers and their desire to "have it all." In doing so, they put in eighty-hour workweeks and raised the first generation of "latchkey" kids, now known as Generation X. When it came time for GenXers to take on the parenting role, they rebelled against their Boomer parents' disciplinarian attitudes and workaholic tendencies. Many GenX women have chosen to be stay- at-home moms while both parents have "befriended" their children and are very involved in their lives.

Is either generation right or wrong? No. But it is interesting how we as a society tend to never let the pendulum remain in the middle. While Boomers may have swung the pendulum too far on discipline and strict authority, the GenXers in many cases swung the pendulum too far the other way, becoming "buddies" with their children. This often leaves the millennial kids, who are typically ages eight to twelve today, lacking when it comes to respect for authority, work ethic, and conflict resolution. Underwood explains that Boomers and some GenXers grew up playing sandlot ball, where kids would fight, argue, and leave the sandlot still best friends by the end of the day. When millennial children in their organized sports leagues have conflicts, they look ten feet away for mom or dad to resolve the problem—or make it worse.

Both generations have worked so hard to give more to their children. Both wanted to make things better for the next generation. But no generation has yet learned the need for balance. Excess of anything—discipline, permissiveness, material possessions, poverty, protectiveness—leads to psychological and emotional imbalance later in life. Effective parenting should lie somewhere in the middle. Of course, Underwood's research was not intended to be a parenting guide, nor does he imply that all people in a generation make the same mistakes. But the patterns are there, like it or not.

> **Boomers:** *The generation born between 1946 and 1964.*
> **Gen X:** *The generation born between 1965 and 1980.*
> **Gen Y:** *The generation born between 1981 and 2000.*
> **Millennials:** *The generation born starting in 2000.*

In today's culture, grasping for the next rung on the ladder of success has become our national sport. This may change with the deepening economic crisis, but as this book was being written, most of us were still in that state of mind. For example, an elderly couple was reviewing the family photo album one day. The wife slowly flipped through the pages with smiles, an occasional tear, and laughter as she relived precious moments in her life. The husband was perplexed as he looked through the album, longing to feel some of the pleasure his wife was experiencing. Where was he? He was not in most of the photos. The few where he did appear showed a disconnected man, there only in body.

When he asked his wife about it, she looked at him for a moment and said, "Do you really not know? Dear, we tried so hard to get you to stop and enjoy life. You were a wonderful provider. We had more than we needed decades ago. But you always wanted more. You were traveling and burning the midnight oil, all to make the next deal, but you missed the biggest deal of all." She said this as she pointed to a photo of a precious five-year-old girl blowing out the candles on a birthday cake with tears streaming down her face. Their daughter. He had missed that birthday and many others. His wife said kindly, "Her fifth birthday wish was for you to be at the party."

A person of significance recognizes the difference between the transitory "treasures" of life and the genuine jewels, and makes the time and thoughtfulness to be a part of the true treasures. Moderation frees us to spend less time working and chasing wealth and more time doing what is truly important to our souls.

Another mistake many Americans make is to substitute giving for time spent pursuing significant passions or relationships. In a report for *Philanthropy*, Gary Tobin, Alex Karp, and Aryeh Weinberg write: "A recent German study reports that on a per capita basis, American citizens contribute to charity nearly seven times as much as their German counterparts, and that about six times as many Americans as Germans do volunteer work. ... Some 70 percent of U.S. households make charitable cash contributions. ... Over half of all U.S. adults will volunteer an estimated twenty billion hours in charitable activities this year. ... In short, American philanthropy is extraordinary by any world standard."

Americans are distinctive not only in the level of their giving, but also in their decentralized and personal nature. Europeans prefer government welfare state transfers. U.S. citizens generally like to give away their money themselves. "Americans give at emergency levels every day," Tobin summarizes in an article about relief efforts for the Dec. 26, 2004, Indian Ocean tsunami disaster. "When the rest of the world has forgotten about this tsunami crisis, Americans will keep giving generously to this and thousands of other causes."

We are not a greedy people. However, consumerism and clever marketing have taken us in to foster discontent with our status in life, and we compensate in the same way: by giving away money rather than spending time with others. People of significance learn to overcome the manipulation toward lives of excess that is a hallmark of modern consumer culture. Jack has learned that concept. He recently retired after twenty-eight years as a driver for his city's sanitation crew. Many may think Jack was not successful. When asked why he didn't pursue other occupations, he said: "I was able to make a living. I took care of my family. We always had food on our table, a roof over our heads, and clothes on our backs. We knew what I made and how much we could spend and that's all we did, and we even managed to save for some rainy days.

"On top of all that, I liked my job. I could whistle all day, listen to the radio, and know I had put in a fair day's work for a fair wage. I never missed my son's football games or my daughter's basketball games. And I always had plenty of love for my beautiful wife when I came home at night. Life has been good to me. I am a blessed man!"

The virtues of simplicity and moderation are part and parcel of significance. Moderate living frees you to spend more of your time with the people you love and make a positive difference in the world. Think, now, how much do you need? Think back to Part One of this book and the discussion of Rome's decline based on overindulgence and "immoderate greatness." If we all could learn to live within our means, we would enjoy excesses of joy in life without needing excesses of "stuff" in life.

7. Authenticity

"Would the real John Smith please stand up?" This was the final line in the TV game show *To Tell the Truth*, which ran from 1956-68. Three contestants would give yes-or-no answers to questions posed by celebrity panelists. Two of the three contestants were imposters. The contests would try to convince the celebrities they were the real person of notoriety. Each wrong vote cast by a celebrity generated money for the contestant. The tension mounted at the end of each round, as all three would rise upon the command to reveal who was the genuine person.

Do you sometimes feel like you are playing that game show in your life? Do your answers to questions depend on who's doing the asking? Are you afraid to stand up for a core belief, the real you, because you would reveal you had been playing the role of imposter all along? So many times in corporate circles or social settings, we wear an appropriate mask for the occasion. We are concerned that if our "real" self is revealed, we may jeopardize our standing among peers. What a sad way to live. When you live that way, you turn yourself into the tool of others. You deny your true passions and lie to yourself about what makes life worth living. You commit that greatest of all sins: *self-deception*. People of significance never allow the opinion of others to dictate their worth, values, or behavior.

Of course, doing this is much easier said than done. When you get pressure from a top client to chair a committee, make a contribution, or take on an extra project, it is tough to say no. But why do you say yes? Are you choosing to say yes because of fear? Are you afraid the other person will think less of you? Are you afraid you will lose the business? Fear should never be a motive for taking on an action or activity that is outside the realm of your core set of beliefs. From the perspective of significance, there should be only one motivation for you to do anything:

Because it aligns with your core values and your beliefs about what is important.

What if your core beliefs call you to an action that may not be viewed well by others? What if you are deeply conflicted about an injustice, but are paralyzed from acting out of fear that others would not approve? People of significance take stands that may appear risky or foolish to one who does not understand the meaning of living by a core set of values. In our society of politically correct behaviors, some of the instances have decreased, but undertones of bias, racism, and hatred still exist. When you stand for a principle according to your values, you make yourself a target. Take it as a sign that you are on the right track!

The abolitionist movement comes to mind as an example of people who were willing to stand up for their authentic beliefs in the face of great peril. Imagine the pressure placed upon those who were convinced of the injustice of slavery. The Underground Railroad was a network of Southerners who were committed to helping slaves escape from their bondage in the South to pursue freedom in the North. Imagine the fear of having Confederate soldiers search your home looking for runaway slaves while ten slaves are crammed into a space behind a false wall. Imagine the scrutiny and outrage you would face as a business owner who funded and assisted in the organization of such networks. Such was the case for Thomas Garrett.

Garrett's hardware store in Wilmington, Delaware, served as the final stop on the Underground Railroad. His Quaker upbringing and core values were the foundation for his support of the abolitionist movement. He was passionate about helping people attain the same freedoms he enjoyed. But according to the Fugitive Slave Act, slaves were property, and anyone helping slaves escape was transporting stolen property across state lines. Federal marshals were vigilant in the enforcement of this act. Slave owners in the South could use the state's power to apprehend and prosecute those who gave a slave passage to freedom.

Garrett was credited with helping more than two thousand people attain passage to freedom. His courageous acts often jeopardized his business and his life, but he always stood proud and defiant in the face of his accusers. He was once apprehended and prosecuted, and the court ordered him to pay a fine of five thousand dollars, a small fortune in those days, to a slave owner for loss of property. The ruling almost bankrupted Garrett. The sheriff admonished him after the trial. "Thomas," he said, "I hope you will never be caught at this again." After a brief silence, Garrett replied, "Friend, I haven't a dollar in the world, but if thee knows of a fugitive anywhere on the face of the earth who needs a breakfast, send him to me." Garrett rebuilt his business to be even stronger and able to help more slaves.

Garrett lived to see the end of slavery before his death in 1871. During his funeral procession, the streets were lined with blacks and whites paying respect to a man who helped them work together to bring freedom to those in bondage. Thousands gathered to watch black pallbearers carry his coffin into the church for his Quaker funeral. He had harbored them into safety and provided food and clothing for their journey to freedom. This last act was a way they could carry him to the freedom of his eternal home and final stop on the railroad of life.

What are you willing to stand for? Does anyone know? Do you know?

Significance Story

In 1959, Ted Williams was closing out his career with the Boston Red Sox, and suffering from a pinched nerve in his neck that season. "The thing was so bad," he later explained, "that I could hardly turn my head to look at the pitcher."

For the first time in his career, he batted under .300, hitting just .254 with ten home runs. He was the highest-salaried player in sports, making $125,000. The next year, the Red Sox sent him the same contract.

When he got the contract, Williams sent it back with a note saying he would not sign it until they gave him the full pay cut allowed, something that's unthinkable today. "I was always treated fairly by the Red Sox when it came to contracts," Williams said. "Now they were offering me a contract I didn't deserve. And I only wanted what I deserved."

Williams cut his own salary by 25 percent, raised his batting average by sixty-two points, and closed out a brilliant career by hitting a home run his final time at bat.

Significance Exercise #10: The Seven Keys

The Seven Keys are the most important qualities in your quest to become a significant individual. This exercise, like #6, asks three people who know you well and can be objective to rate you in these seven areas. You will learn about the paths you must walk to achieve a life of splendid significance.

Ask three people who know you very well and will be honest with you to rate you on the Seven Keys on a scale of one to ten, with ten being the most favorable. Use the descriptions for each listed below so they understand what you're asking.

Unconditional Love The ability to love and cherish each person without judgment	**Spontaneous Generosity** Giving without an expectation of thanks or recognition	**Appreciation of Solitude** The ability to set things aside, quiet the mind and "be"
First person's rating:	First person's rating:	First person's rating:
Second person's rating:	Second person's rating:	Second person's rating:
Third person's rating:	Third person's rating:	Third person's rating:
Average of the three:	Average of the three:	Average of the three:
_____	_____	_____

Passion Being willing to invest time and energy doing that which brings you joy	**Learning and Mentoring** Listening and learning from the wisdom of others and passing on what you know	**Moderation** Appreciation for simplicity and thrift and the perspective that not everyone is as fortunate as you
First person's rating:	First person's rating:	First person's rating:
Second person's rating:	Second person's rating:	Second person's rating:
Third person's rating:	Third person's rating:	Third person's rating:
Average of the three:	Average of the three:	Average of the three:
_____	_____	_____

Authenticity Being who you are rather than creating a false persona to impress others	**Scoring (your average for each Key)**	
First person's rating: Second person's rating: Third person's rating: Average of the three: _____	8-10: This Key is a strength for you, and one of the foundations of your pursuit of significance. 5-7: You have a strong base to build on and improve this Key to where it becomes a source of joy and meaning. 1-4: This is a weakness. I advise you to spend some time talking to the people who answered these questions and ask them why they rated you this way, then discern choices you can make to develop this Key and improve your score.	

You will not achieve significance until you have learned to:

- Love unconditionally.
- Give spontaneously.
- Seek solitude.
- Follow your passion.
- Learn and mentor others.
- Practice moderation.
- Be your authentic self.

Rely on the exercise above, the truthful feedback of others, and your own experiences to begin making a plan to improve places in the Seven Keys where you are weakest. An improvement in even one will bring you closer to significance.

Next Steps for Significance Seekers...

- *... Give unconditional love to someone who needs it desperately, like a homeless person.*

- *... Take the money out of your wallet right now, go to the nearest charity or nonprofit, and donate it, no questions asked. How did it feel?*

- *... Spend as much time as you can during a day in silence; no music, no TV, no conversation, no talking to yourself. Enjoy the silence and how it changes your thoughts.*

- *... Pick something you've been passionate about for a long time but never pursued, such as playing the piano, and start pursuing it.*

- *... Go to www.mentoring.org and learn about becoming a mentor.*

- *... Practice moderation by giving up something permanently.*

- *... Drop at least one pretense that you have maintained only to impress others.*

CHAPTER SEVEN
Practical Significance

All the interests of my reason, speculative as well as practical, combine in the three following questions: 1. What can I know? 2. What ought I to do? 3. What may I hope?

—*Immanuel Kant, German philosopher*

Jim Sinegal is a CEO who has realized unprecedented success in the fickle and challenging retail business. Costco, founded in 1983 as Price Club, is a $72 billion discount warehouse chain with 544 stores in forty states. Jim's business model is deep-discount while selling high volume, and millions of Americans adore his company. But more importantly, Jim has built the company on the bedrock of his significant, practical, real-world values.

The son of a steel worker, he started in the warehouse business unloading mattresses. Throughout his career, he has maintained strong working-class values. He said in an interview for the news show *20/20* that he actually *likes* his employees. His philosophy is, "If you obey the law, take care of your customers, and take care of your people, if you do these things, you will reward your shareholders." A humble man, he wears a name tag with his first name only—no title and no status. He answers his own phone and sends out his own faxes, and his office furniture consists of a banquet table and a folding chair.

The key to Jim Sinegal's success is that he has never lost sight of the importance of people, and that has made him a significant force in improving people's lives and setting an example for American business. Jim visits up to a dozen Costco stores per day. He says, "No manager, no staff feels good if the boss isn't interested enough to come and see them." In an era when some corporations are being demonized for getting rich on the backs of poorly paid workers without healthcare, Costco is revered because it pays healthy wages—about seventeen dollars per hour, well above average for retail—provides healthcare to everyone, and cares for its employees in many smaller ways.

For this, Jim has drawn criticism from Wall Street, which says he could make more money if he paid less in wages. He doesn't see it that way. Costco also promotes from within to fill almost 100 percent of its positions. There are vice presidents in the company who started as employees bringing in grocery carts. As a result of all of these things, the company has the lowest turnover rate in retail, saving it millions a year in recruitment and training costs.

And, what about Jim's CEO salary? Excessive, right? Wrong. Although he runs a $72 billion business, he pays himself just $350,000 per year, a fraction of most CEO salaries. He says he figured if he made about twelve times the average wage of the person on the floor, then that would be fair. And, most unbelievably, he has a *one-page* employment contract that states he can be terminated for cause. If he doesn't perform, he's out the door.

This does not mean Costco is immune to the challenges within the domestic and global economy. But Jim and his management team tackle all of these challenges with the same verve and values they bring to everyday business challenges. For instance, until the economic collapse, soaring commodities prices forced manufacturers around the world to raise the prices they charge retailers, who passed them along to consumers. Yet Costco cannot raise prices as easily as its rivals; about three-quarters of its operating profits come from membership fees, and if it were to hike prices too high, shoppers would let their memberships expire and profits could suffer.

So Jim did what he does best: crank up Costco's highly aggressive cost-cutting machine to new levels. This did not mean layoffs as it would in many organizations. He challenged managers to find ways to pare costs. For example, after Proctor & Gamble announced a 6 percent price hike on Bounty paper towels and Charmin toilet tissue, Costco bought hundreds of truckloads at the old price and stuffed them into storage depots, saving customers precious pennies per roll. The company has even looked into growing its own pumpkins to help preserve the $5.99 price tag on its store-baked pies. Jim says, "If that stuff doesn't really turn you on, then you're in the wrong business."

Let's close this story with one last philosophy from Jim: "Treat workers like family, treat customers like guests, and when you are the boss—be a regular guy." Jim Sinegal is a man who has proved success does not have to mean sacrificing his personal values. He has found his path to significance.

Cause and Effect

That story is a fantastic example of tremendous practical benefits—in this case, to millions—coming about because of one person's adherence to his significant principles. Jim could have chosen to pursue the narrow path of financial success by raising prices and laying people off; that probably would have raised the Costco share price and made Jim richer for a while. But in the end, the shallow pursuit of success could have wrecked the company. Through the practical application of significant principles, Jim has created something rare: a significant company.

> ***Significant company:*** *An organization that, through its policies, has a beneficial effect on the community, society, or the world while also achieving business and fiscal success.*

That is exactly what you are seeking as you move along the path to significance: a practical application for the principles you've learned about, the Seven Pillars and the Seven Keys. After all, what good are theoretical principles if you can't turn them into something that makes a difference in the real world? That would have been like Benjamin Franklin discovering the principles of electricity but Thomas Edison never inventing the light bulb. Fortunately, there are many ways you can achieve "practical significance." In fact, that is the point of this book. I want to share with you insights and actions that can turn your own significant qualities into tangible, lasting, positive change in your life, and from there into the lives of others.

The goal is not only to discover you can have significance as well as success in your life, but that significance can actually become the fuel for your financial and professional success—that by building your life around the Seven Keys and living according to your essence and passion, you will inspire others to work with you and you will attract opportunities, earn incredible loyalty, and find in yourself a creative fire and problem-solving energy you might not know you have. Significance becomes a top-down competitive advantage, a secret weapon for transforming your career, your relationships ... your entire life. The pursuit of significance is the cause that sets good things in motion; the joy and compassion and fulfillment you will find are the effect. And it all begins with practical steps taken today, right now.

But first, we need to ask a question together: What do you want?

Find the Pain

Marketing consultant Chuck McCay writes that pain is the key to successful marketing. Basically, he says, unless you can find the customer's pain or convince that person he or she is in pain and that your brand will relieve it, you can't sell anything. The pain doesn't have to be physical, of course. It could be anything from a dwindling retirement account to a car that gets bad gas mileage. The key is that if there is a need, there must also exist a solution for that need. But you can't sell—or buy—the solution until you know the need exists.

The idea of unknown pain is incredibly relevant to the practical side of significance. I'll illustrate with a story about Scott, a man in his forties. For years, like many people, Scott had shrugged off the idea of doctors and healthcare. He'd go for a physical every seven years or so, but beyond that, he didn't think much about his health. As a result, he slowly gained a few pounds a year until he was about forty pounds overweight, though he didn't realize it. Denial is a powerful thing.

When he turned forty, Scott's wife prevailed upon him to go in for a physical. When he did, he was stunned to find out his blood pressure and cholesterol were quite high, putting him at a seriously elevated risk for a heart attack. Scott was shocked by this; he hadn't even paid attention to the weight gain, but it was obviously responsible for his bad numbers. He had a problem—a pain—that he hadn't even known about. Without knowing about it, he hadn't been able to address it.

That changed after his physical. Scott had no interest in being a statistic. He got on blood pressure medication as a precaution, but immediately started a workout and healthy eating program. In just three months, he shocked his doctor by dropping more than twenty pounds and getting his cholesterol into the safe range. In a year, he had dropped forty-five pounds and quit the blood pressure medication. Today, at forty-four, he's in the best shape of his life ... all because he learned about a pain he didn't know was even an issue.

Odds are, you are the same way in your life, suffering with a pain you may not even recognize or want to admit. As human beings, we fear pain and sometimes even see it as a sign of weakness. We shouldn't. Pain is the body's natural defense mechanism; it's the body's way of saying something is not right and that we should pay attention. Instead of closing our minds to it and hoping it will go away, we should consider pain an ally. Your pain, like your feeling of fear, serves a natural purpose in awakening the senses that help keep you alive.

Yet inertia is a powerful force, compelling us to stick with what we're doing even when it's hurting us, because our fear of change is greater than our fear of what might happen in ten or twenty years. The simple truth is, if you are reading this book you are likely in pain in one or more of the four central zones of life:

Career

Family

Community

Creativity

In one or more of these areas, it's very likely you are feeling stunted, empty, stressed out, and lost, as though there was an exit off life's highway that you were supposed to take but missed because you were so busy chasing the dollar. That is pain—the pain of a life that could have been but is not. You are trapped in the prison of compromises you have made in order to pursue shallow success at the expense of your essence of being.

It's time to break out of that prison and get back on the road to the life you should have had, the life you can still have. But first, you must admit to yourself that what you're doing now isn't working. In fact, it's causing you emotional, mental, and spiritual agony. We'll start this enlightening process of self-discovery with an exercise. In it, you'll answer four questions that will give you greater insight into yourself than you may have thought possible.

Significance Exercise #11: Find the Pain

You can't get treated until you know what disease you have. Similarly, you can't make core changes to your life until you know the areas of your life that are causing you pain. This is your "pain detector."

Identify the two areas of your life (choosing from Career, Family, Community, and Creativity) where you feel the greatest anxiety, emptiness, regret, or stress. For each, answer the four questions.

Painful area #1:

What about this area causes you pain?

What could you do differently to align this part of your life with your essence?

What's stopping you?

Painful area #2:

What about this area causes you pain?

What could you do differently to align this part of your life with your essence?

What's stopping you?

Heading Down Another Street

It's important to note that if you're in major pain in two areas of life, you're probably in some pain in the others as well. It's hard to be a significant, world-changing dad and husband while you're slaving away at a career you've grown to hate. The ennui and regret of meaningless success spread like a tumor to all parts of your life. The important thing is to find the areas where the empty quest for success is causing you the most pain and transform them. Then the others will change for the better.

Once you have identified your pain, which could also be described as areas of your life that are afflicted with significancer, then you have to face up to the most difficult question of all:

Do you believe your pain will cease if you continue to do things the same way?

There is a self-help parable that goes like this: A woman is walking down a street riddled with deep potholes. She knows she should go another way, but this street is familiar. Not long after setting out, she falls into a hole. She's perplexed, but she claws her way out and continues on her merry way. A few minutes later, she falls into another, deeper hole. Now's she's irritated; she should have seen this one and avoided it. She clambers out, dusts herself off, and stubbornly continues walking up the street.

This goes on for hours. The woman tumbles into progressively deeper and deeper holes, getting more and more angry about it, pulls herself out, and keeps walking. Finally, she falls into the deepest hole yet. She knows she's going to get filthy climbing out, and she's furious at herself. "This is ridiculous," she thinks. "I can't keep doing this." She slowly crawls to the street, gets up, dusts herself off, gets her things in order … and walks up a different street.

The potholes are the traps we set for our significance as we chase the easy, the superficial, and the socially acceptable. When we realize that in these areas of life we can be not only happy but find meaning, service, connection, and true joy, we turn up a different street and make changes in our choices. We orient toward significance and realize we can no longer do things the way we once did. It is no longer acceptable to work eighty-hour weeks, run up massive credit card debt trying to keep up with our friends, miss our kids' soccer games, or leave the guitar we love gathering dust in the closet. We suddenly see we deserve more, can be more, can do so much more.

I don't claim to be able to guide you to that "aha" moment, as some therapists call it. That is truly up to you. My goal is to give you the insight, questions, and tools so when you come to the point where you are ready to head down the street of significance in the neglected areas of your life, you will know what to do.

> ***Aha moment:*** *That moment of enlightenment when you see clearly the mistakes you have made and what you must do to realize your full potential.*

Practical Significance Solutions

We're going to take a closer look at the six main areas of life from a "significance versus success" perspective so you can see how to apply the lessons of the Seven Keys to Significance in your everyday life and bring more love, generosity, moderation, authenticity, passion, learning, and solitary peace into each day. We'll look at the following facts:

1. *The three most common examples of "significancer" in each area*
2. *The symptoms*
3. *Practical things you can do today to move toward significance and increase your Significance Quotient*

1. Career

Career pursuits are probably the number one narcotic that draws people away from significance toward the shallow side of success. It is apparently easy to succumb to the draw of position, status, challenge, and financial reward. Of course, this is understandable; all of us want to achieve something important on a professional level, and it can be quite an ego boost to be deeply involved in a stimulating pursuit such as building a company, creating an innovation, or transforming an industry. But for many people, the initial excitement is just a "gateway drug." The novelty of career challenge soon becomes a constant striving for more and more—more money, status, perks, or simply more hours to satisfy the demands of a power structure that doesn't know you or care about you.

But career is a harsh master. It drives us to neglect everything else with the promise that if we work *just* this much longer, sacrifice *just* so much more, we'll have all the security, admiration, and love we could ever want. And once we are walking on the treadmill of our careers, we're likely to stay on them. After all, we probably have a mortgage, car payments, credit card bills, and other obligations that depend on uninterrupted income. The stress of the unmitigated pursuit of career has turned prestigious professions into traps in many cases. A November 2008 survey of more than twelve thousand physicians conducted by the Physicians' Foundation found that nearly 50 percent of primary care doctors in the United States were planning to cut back the number of patients they saw or quit medicine altogether. About 60 percent said they would not recommend medicine as a career.

Is your career blocking your path toward significance? It is if you experience one or more of these "significancerous" situations:

1. You feel like work dominates every day, including weekends and vacations.
2. You're missing out on the "other" parts of life like children's activities, vacations, and personal downtime—in fact, that you think of them as "other" in the first place speaks volumes.
3. You have built up such a large amount of debt that you feel trapped into working endlessly to pay for your material possessions, but you get little pleasure from them.

Like Randy in the story from Chapter One, if you're in this position, your career has become your life. Instead of living with significance, you spend all your time, energy, and passion meeting the expectations of others; there's simply nothing left to think about giving to help someone else. You're used up by your work. Symptoms of this form of significancer include:

- Constant stress.
- The feeling that there's never enough time in the day.
- Isolation from family and friends.
- The feeling that you're on a treadmill leading nowhere.

What are some of the solutions you can explore to bring yourself more in balance between success and significance and take back your life from your work without necessarily quitting your job (though that might prove to be the best course of action for some people)? Think about some of these practical options:

- Find a meaningful cause you can fit into your schedule, like Jim giving blood regularly.
- Develop a charitable giving idea that can be integrated into your company's business model.
- Develop a plan to pay down your debt so you can afford to work fewer hours.
- Draft a plan to work from home several days a week, allowing you to reduce your commute and have more opportunities to be with your family.
- Examine your job for ways you can streamline or delegate tasks to give you some breathing room.
- Work solitude or meditation time into each day.

All of these suggestions are really addressing the symptoms, not the disease. What's the disease? Not having enough time or mental energy to do anything but work, even if there are causes or pleasures about which you care immensely. Once you free some of your precious time from your career, you'll be amazed at what you can achieve. Remember, time is more precious than money, because you can always get more money, but you can't get more time.

A great example of turning aside from pure career success toward significance is the story of Patrick and Jean Smith. As told in the book *Turning Dreams into Success* by Bunny and Larry Holman, Patrick was owner and president of a Fortune 500 company, Software Information Systems, until 1998. It was a highly successful company and consumed all of his time. Then in 1997 and 1998, Patrick and Jean went on a Habitat for Humanity mission to Africa to build houses and a church in the village of Assasan, Ghana. That changed everything. In 1999, they sold their interest in the company to fulfill their new mission of working to create a better life for the Ghanans they had come to love.

They launched a business called Global HandWorks to fund projects of homeowners in Africa and allow them to make a living off their handicrafts, funneling part of the money to the local Habitat affiliate, allowing more houses to be built. The Smiths say they have never felt happier, more purposeful, or more "successful" than they have since they stopped climbing the ladder of traditional success and dedicating their lives to others.

A son and his father were walking in the mountains. Suddenly, the son fell, hurt himself, and screamed: "Ahh!"

To his surprise, he heard a voice repeating, somewhere in the mountains: "Ahh!"

Curious, he yelled: "Who are you?" The answer: "Who are you?"

Angered, he screamed: "Coward!" The answer: "Coward!"

He looked to his father and asked, "What's going on?"

The father smiled and said, "My son, pay attention."

Then the father screamed to the mountain, "I admire you!" The voice answered: "I admire you!"

Again the man screamed, "You are a champion!" The voice came back: "You are a champion!"

The boy was surprised but did not understand.

The father explained: "People call this an echo, but really this is life. It gives you back everything you say or do. Our life is simply a reflection of our actions. If you want more love in the world, create more love in your heart. If you want more competence in your team, improve your competence. This relationship applies to everything, in all aspects of life. Life will give you back everything you have given to it."

Your life is not a coincidence. It is a reflection of you.

Family

Family frequently pays the price for the overzealous pursuit of career and financial success. Why is it so easy for us to take our loved ones for granted? I don't know the answer, but I do know it's all too common. There's the story of a successful speaker and coach who spent hundreds of days per year on the road. When he got home at last, his kids were distant and resentful. Finally, he asked them what he could do differently, explaining he had to travel and be gone a lot so their family could afford their nice house and the kids' private school. His daughter, with that wisdom children so often display, said, "I understand, Daddy. But when you're here, I want you to really *be* here."

This was devastating, because the man realized that even when he was home from his grueling road schedule, he was often on the phone, at his computer, or writing speeches. He wasn't devoting the majority of his time to the people who were supposed to be the most important in his life, his wife and children. Chastened and upset at himself, he vowed to do better, and set up a system where he would track the hours he spent with his kids when he was home to ensure they were getting quantity and quality time.

I think it is so easy to take family for granted because, as with our health, we take notice only when something is wrong. Unless there's a disaster, it's easy to assume the family unit will run on autopilot and say, "I'll go to the next dance recital." Over the long term, the slights and absences add up to a wound that cannot be healed. At the least, you have a family unit that's distant and cold, not giving anyone the love and support it takes to thrive and be significant. At worst, you have divorce, pain, anger, and division, lives shattered. The most common forms of this kind of significancer:

1. Communication shutdown
2. Constant conflict
3. Separation or divorce
4. Infidelity

Family troubles don't have to be about career. They can also be the product of grudges or other issues that have built up over the years. Why does this affect your significance? Because family—whether it's the spouse and kids, siblings, your parents, your entire extended family— is the anchor for each of us in life. In a world that can be cold and heartless, we come home to family to recharge, to be reminded we are worthy of love. In the best of situations, family members become part of our striving for significance. Our children inspire us to work to help other children. Perhaps we work extra hours so our spouse can pursue his or her labor of love in music or writing. Family is the center of our being; it reminds us who we are and what we're living for.

So when family life is diseased, it manifests in some of these ways:

- You dread time with family because of the guilt you feel at neglecting them.
- You constantly argue.
- You miss special event after special event.
- You buy the kids extra "goodies" to compensate for not being there.

All of us have made family sacrifices in one way or another because of our work. There's nothing wrong with that. The trouble comes when choosing work over family becomes the rule, not the exception. To achieve significance, balance is mandatory—between work and play, effort and restoration, giving and being the recipient. The most powerful force in your life to keep you balanced, at peace, and charged with love and a sense of purpose is your family.

These are some practical ideas for bringing significance into your family situation, thus bringing yourself closer to the proper balance:

- Carve out "family periods" in your busy schedule, times when you do nothing that isn't related to giving your family your undivided attention.
- Talk openly about past transgressions such as missed events, lack of communication, or betrayals of trust.
- Invite your family members to be part of your work by taking your children to the office or giving your spouse a role in a personal project.
- Create a "cause" that all family members can participate in, such as feeding the homeless or raising money for a charity.

Family is the platform from which all significance springs. Yours will be your source of strength and inspiration, the cure for self-doubt, and the environment in which the lessons you learn working to benefit others and the community come back to you multiplied many times. You just have to see what family can be.

Significance Story

From Bob McCauley:

Twenty-four years ago, I started AmeriCares, a relief organization that distributes critical medicines and medical supplies to the world's poor in times of disaster. Since then we've distributed five billion dollars in aid to people in 137 countries. It's an amazing number. I can't quite believe it. But maybe I shouldn't be surprised. I often had to raise that money myself (I've gone begging to some of the biggest corporate CEOs). I had to learn to be a beggar—and I learned from the very best.

"Bub," she called me. With her thick Albanian accent, she could never quite pronounce my name. She was tiny, of course—not even five feet—but not frail. And she never slowed down. I have a photo of the two of us walking together on the tarmac at some airport, my hand at her back. People who've seen it have said, "You seem to be giving Mother Teresa a hand there." I tell them the truth: "I've got my hand on her back to slow her down. I couldn't keep up."

My lesson about begging came on a commercial flight. We'd visited several orphanages in Guatemala and were heading on Taca Airlines to Mexico City. AmeriCares was still in its infancy and I was wondering how to grow it. I'd had plenty of experience fund-raising but I'd still get self-conscious going to someone, hat in hand. It was for a good cause, but how should I ask? Just then the flight attendant brought us our lunches. "Excuse me," Mother Teresa said. "How much does this meal cost?"

The flight attendant shrugged. "I don't know. About one dollar in U.S. currency." I'm sure this was a question no passenger had ever asked.

"If I give it back to you," Mother said, "would you give me that dollar to give to the poor?"

The flight attendant looked startled. "I don't know if I can," she stammered. "It's not something we normally do." I put down my fork. The flight attendant left her cart and went to the front of the plane to consult with the pilot. A few minutes latter she returned to us. "Yes, Mother," she said. "You may have the money for the poor."

"Here you are." Mother Teresa handed her tray. I gave her mine, too. No way could I eat in peace with Mother next to me. I could do without a meal or two anyway. Then I noticed the fellow across the aisle handing his tray to the attendant. The couple in front did the same. The attendant started down the aisle. Suddenly it seemed no one on that flight wanted to eat lunch. The flight attendant got the

speaker and said, "If anyone gives up their meal, the airline will give one dollar to Mother Teresa for the poor."

Can you believe it? Not a soul wanted lunch on that flight, including the crew. I stood up and counted. There were 129 people on board. "Pretty good," I said to Mother. "Now you've got $129 for the poor."

She was not finished. "Bub," she said when the plane landed, "get me the food."

"What are you going to do with 129 airline lunches?"

"They can't use them now. We can give them to the poor." With some reluctance I went to the airline officials who were gathered on the tarmac to greet Mother Teresa. There was much handshaking and then I got to the point: "Thanks for giving us money for the lunches. … Mother Teresa would like to know if she could have the lunches too?" What were we going to do with 129 trays of food? Put them in the trunk of a taxi and drive off?

The officials conferred. "Of course," one man said with a courtly bow. "Anything Mother wishes." I walked back to Mother Teresa to tell her the good news.

She hardly paused for breath. "Bub," she said, "get me the truck."

"What?" I wasn't sure I'd heard her right.

"I want the truck." A few minutes later, I was sitting in the passenger seat of a Taca Airlines truck with a diminutive nun behind the wheel. She was so short she had to peer between the steering wheel and dashboard to see. "Where are we going?" I asked.

"To the poor." It was a hair-raising trip. She was a terrible driver—it was only by the grace of God she didn't hit another vehicle. In a half-hour we found ourselves in one of those desperately poor Mexican neighborhoods of cardboard shanties. She pulled over to the side of the road. A swarm of kids gathered around us. Their parents followed. Mother Teresa leaped to the ground and opened the back of the truck, handing out meals. The recipients had no idea who she was. They just knew she had food.

The truck, the lunches, the money—how had she gotten it all? By asking. Come to think of it, she'd had me do most of the asking. We got back into the truck and headed back to the airport. "Bub," she said, "it's easy to ask when you're doing it for the poor." And for twenty-four years it has been. God can give you the power to do anything—even beg shamelessly—when you're doing it for the people who need it the most.

Community

Community can be anything from your church to the local charity group or food bank—anything that affects the lives of multiple people beyond you and your family. Habitat for Humanity is part of the community—in this case, the community of all mankind, of which we are all members. When we reach out to work at our church teaching Bible study to youngsters, serve food at a local soup kitchen during the holidays, plant trees to prevent climate change, or go into schools to educate students about the importance of giving blood, we are building our significance in the community.

Community can benefit from success in the form of money given as donations, usually because of the tax deduction. There's nothing wrong with that; it would be naïve to think nonprofit organizations care about the motives of the people who give them money. However, if all you do is give money to some charity or community group to assuage your guilt over working too hard and not doing enough personally to make a difference, how does that help you? Your significance is a charity in itself, and it needs to be fed like a delicate plant. Significance blooms on a diet of selfless giving, compassion, and hard work on behalf of those less fortunate than yourself. If you are giving money earned in the relentless race for success while neglecting to reach out and make human contact with people or causes that need you, you are cheating yourself. That's not significance. That's self-delusion. Anyone can write a check.

Yes, financial support matters. So give, but do more. Reach out. Connect with the community. Research has shown human altruism, which evolutionary biologists have tried to explain away as a trait that somehow contributed to natural selection, cannot be so easily written off to survival of the fittest. It's hard to explain, but one possibility is that we do good because it feels wonderful. Ask yourself how it felt the last time you did something generous for someone, or aided a person in need. It made you glow, didn't it? It made you feel like Bob McCauley traveling with Mother Teresa: blessed to be a blessing to others. When you feel that way, you are significant.

When you don't, several kinds of significancer could be to blame:

1. You give money as an excuse to avoid having to give of your time.
2. You block out all information about community causes, organizations, and problems that need solving.
3. You lump the needy or troubled into neat groups, using terms like "those people" and making broad assumptions about their unworthiness to justify your refusal to get involved.

Community atrophies when people don't give or care, and thrives when they share their time, expertise, commitment, physical labor, and love to make good things happen. If you are not participating in the development of your community in some way, you are not on the path to significance. Remember, significance means improving the state of the world for others; you cannot do that if you refuse to open to the needs around you. The efforts need not be dramatic, but you must reach out. Not doing so can lead to these symptoms:

- Resentment of the guilt you feel for not pitching in.
- Isolation from other members of the community.
- Stress that comes from assuming your problems are the worst in the world.
- A feeling of emptiness and lack of direction.
- Problems in your community going unsolved.

Simply adopting a spirit of outreach and change can turn even the humblest person into a force for dynamic improvement in the lives of many. For example, a group of residents of Portland, Oregon, were dismayed to see that no one in their neighborhood spoke to one another and cars zipped through at dangerous speeds. Rather than try to get laws passed—an obstructive method of bringing about change—they decided to band together to bring about creative change. Working with dozens of adults and children from the surrounding area, they decided to turn one four-way residential intersection into a neighborhood hub, painting it with an elaborate mural and erecting coffee carts, a self-service library, a message kiosk, and more on the sidewalks around the intersection.

The idea was a smashing success. Cars slowed to investigate. People started hanging out and chatting at the kiosk and exchanging books at the library. More services and mini-booths followed. A few years later, this small project has blossomed into the principles known as City Repair and is spreading to urban areas all over the country. All because some folks from the neighborhood cared enough to band together, get creative, and do something. What can you do to make a difference and advance your Significance Quotient? Here are some ideas:

- Become a mentor to a child in need.
- Take a position of responsibility at your church.
- Become a fundraiser for a worthy organization in your town.
- Hold a political or advocacy-related event at your home.
- Collect needed goods for the poor.
- Dedicate one day per month to addressing a problem in your community.
- Volunteer for a board or committee.

- Attend a city council meeting where public feedback is invited on a vital issue.
- Use your business skills to help a group improve its operations or become financially healthier.

A warning: This can become addictive. Once you reach out in a small way and start bringing significance into the lives of others, you may not want to stop. It feels incredible. You will discover a new family of people who care and share the same glow you have. You'll also find a new sense of purpose. This is one addiction that couldn't be healthier.

> ***Creative change:*** *Transforming a situation not by restricting activity or stopping people from doing something, but by creatively changing the environment, goals, or style of activity.*

Creativity

Think about painters. Musicians. Gardeners. Poets. How do they serve the world and create significance? Aren't they simply indulging a deep passion for creation? Yes, but in doing so they create works of joy and beauty, and those works bring joy and warmth to the world. That's significant. If you are earning a living from a place of pure passion and delight, doing something you would do if you never received a dime, you are on a significant path. It all depends on your motive.

Is there something you have always wanted to do but did not pursue because it wasn't practical as a career? Most of us do, and it's typically something creative. We all crave the feeling of creation, because that is our link to God. All humans are creators in their essence of being. Some create music, art, or verse. Others create buildings, characters on stage, or films. Still others create crafts, furniture, inventions, or even businesses. Many of the most worthwhile endeavors of the human enterprise are creative. You probably have a creative soul inside you bursting to get out. Think about it. What have you always wanted to do, even if you've never told anyone about it? What do you hunger to create?

The significant person is a sum of many parts, and one of them is personal joy. If you feel filled with happiness because you are engaged, even as a hobby, in something that brings you joy, you are more likely to spread that good feeling to others around you through good works. Is that not true? I have certainly found it to be the case. The most significant people didn't find their happiness by their acts of generosity and compassion—they already shone with a light of elation from the other areas of their life, such as family or creativity.

If you are ignoring the call from within you to express your creative impulse, you are stunting your significance. There are several forms of this significancer:

1. You deny any interest in playing the saxophone, writing poetry, or building sailboats.
2. You denigrate creative practices and creative people as impractical and economically worthless.
3. You feel a gnawing regret at what might have been had you not listened to those who told you to "have something to fall back on."

It is definitely in the interest of your significant life path to pursue your development as a complete, joyful, balanced human being, and part of that means expressing that which you have inside you. You don't have to give up your career, though some people do when they find that their pure passion for their creativity means they can do what they love, still make a good living, and lead the life of their dreams. Even if you remain a stockbroker and write short stories on the weekends, fine. You are enriching the world in two ways: You are becoming a more balanced and life-affirming person, and you are adding to the beauty of the world. Remember, art, music, and other forms of creation exist for their own sake, to inspire and elevate us. As John Keats said, "A thing of beauty is a joy forever."

What can happen when you deny that creative voice? These are a few classic symptoms:

- You avoid any contact with the thing you'd love to be doing.
- You get depressed.
- You forget why you do what you do to make a living.
- You blame others for convincing you not to pursue the creative pursuit you love.
- You convince yourself it's "too late."

You can make the time to do what is most important to you, and you should. If it becomes a second career, great. Maybe it can't be a career now but can become one in retirement. Or perhaps it will always be something you dabble in but which gives you pleasure, or perhaps something you teach your children. In any case, the delight you radiate will bring positive energy to everything else you do. You'll find yourself refreshed and renewed at work and at home. Try some of these practical ideas:

- Take a class in your area of interest.
- Find a mentor in the topic, preferably an older person who would thrive on the attention and respect.
- Go on a retreat dedicated to the activity.
- Share your interest with your kids; maybe they have it, too!

Seeking significance is absolutely rejuvenating. A wonderful example of this is Marge Jetton, a former nurse who was profiled in the November 2005 issue of *National Geographic* and then many other publications, including *AARP* in November/December 2008 about her secrets to longevity. Marge had been a proud doctor's wife and adored the work she did to help her husband. When he died suddenly in a tragic fall, she was understandably devastated. It would have been reasonable to expect that she would, as so many people do, follow her spouse to the grave within months.

However, people who thought that obviously didn't know Marge well. She spent a few months grieving, then got back to living: volunteering at her church, raising money for a gospel radio program, and delivering magazines to elderly hospital patients. "I realized that the world wasn't going to come to me, so I went back out into the world," she said in her interview. "I reconnected with old friends and felt satisfaction from helping the community. I guess you could say that I recharged my purpose batteries."

Marge is now 104 years old and still going. She's given up her car, but to save money, not because she can't drive it. She credits her vitality to her religious faith and her belief that she has a purpose and can make a difference. Marge found her significance by putting aside her own grief and focusing on her purpose, and in doing so discovered her essence of being.

Significance Exercise #12: Practical Significance

I have given you some practical, real-world ideas for pursuing significance in four key areas of life. But your circumstances are unique. Can you come up with some new ideas?

For each of the four key areas of life, write down at least three additional things you could do RIGHT NOW to move yourself in the direction of significance.

Career

1.

2.

3.

Family

1.

2.

3.

Community

1.

2.

3.

Creativity

1.

2.

3.

There are as many ways to bring significance into a life as there are people. My ideas may not work for you, but I hope they will inspire some creative thinking. Just remember that understanding the concepts and philosophies behind significance is only half the battle. What will set you on a new course toward meaning, purpose, and a splendid legacy is heartfelt, committed action … and it begins today.

Next Steps for Significance Seekers…

- … *What kind of example are you setting for your children and their ability to follow their own dreams?*

- … *Could you make a living doing what you love that would let you keep your same standard of living? Crunch the numbers. What would you have to do?*

- … *See the experts in action—musicians, artists, athletes, actors. Learn from watching them. Get to know them and pick their brains.*

- … *See if your company has a fellowship or other program encouraging people to pursue creative projects.*

- … *Consider a sabbatical to try your hand at what you love.*

CHAPTER EIGHT
The Seven Attributes of a Significant Leader

KEY ASPECTS OF SIGNIFICANT LEADERSHIP FOR CEOS, ENTREPRENEURS, CIVIC LEADERS, EDUCATORS, AND ANYONE IN A POSITION OF AUTHORITY

If your actions inspire others to dream more, learn more, do more, and become more, you are a leader.

—John Quincy Adams, sixth U.S. president

A Significant Leader is someone who is living his or her "essence of being" and is willing to help and guide others to pursue their own significance. This person leads not through fear or implied authority but by inspiring others. Apart from making sound decisions and staying cool in crisis situations, the hallmark of a great leader—and the requirement for a significant one—is the ability to bring out the best in others.

Once people have begun to live their own "essence of being," they are often compelled to assist others in their pursuit of significance. Those who have success as Significant Leaders often display a common set of attributes they integrate into all of their efforts. Like the Seven Keys to unlocking significance, these qualities are essential to personal development and appear in one form or another in every Significant Leader. However, we face a leadership crisis in this country, as I've already alluded to. In point of fact, we are in danger of going down the same road as ancient Rome—into corruption, sloth, poverty, war, and eventual destruction—unless we can recapture the qualities that make true leaders great. You'll read about them later in this chapter under many names like *character* and *courage*, but what this really comes down to is a single word: *honor*. A major paradigm shift is needed in the way we educate our leaders in our culture, and restoring honor is at its heart. Let's take a look at it.

The Paradigm Shift

After the disaster of Enron in 2001, Congress passed the Sarbanes-Oxley Act, which established tough new financial reporting standards for public corporations, auditors, company boards, and accounting firms. This wiped out major corporate fraud, right? Of course not. Look at the 2008 financial market meltdown and the proliferation of bad loans, pyramid investment scams, and unregulated securities and it's obvious: Sarbanes-Oxley was a Band-Aid on a chest wound.

Yes, we need regulation and sanctions to have a just society, but by themselves they won't change the behavior of people who are oriented toward greed and success at any cost—any more than the threat of arrest and jail will change the behavior of a juvenile raised without any basic moral code. You cannot legislate morality, as we learned with Prohibition. As a result, we have a culture that rewards profit and success at any cost, turning robber baron capitalists and the politicians who cater to them into heroes. And often, CEOs who eschew runaway profits in favor of policies that benefit the environment or the poor lose their jobs or suffer legal action because they did not work to "maximize shareholder value."

In short, we are teaching our leaders to think only of success and to ignore significance unless it can be used as a PR opportunity. This must change. We cannot afford to become Rome; instead, we should be slowly tilting our education of leaders in business schools, law schools,, and political institutions toward honor. I know the word conjures up ancient images, but what is more relevant than honor, a personal moral code that means you can be taken at your word and you will respect the rights and ethics of others? The military tries to teach this, but it is also subject to the "success-first" ethos of our times. What we need is to get back to Confucius' wisdom and find leaders based on their ethics, compassion, and moral compass *as well as* their ability to run an organization.

It is well past time for a new model for teaching young people what it means to be a leader—that it is about making a positive difference and serving that passionate purpose inside yourself, not just about making money. Writing for the Corporate Responsibility Officer blog, Neil Smith says as much:

In the foreword of Authentic Leadership, *author Bill George, former CEO of Medtronic, writes, "We need … people of the highest integrity, committed to building enduring organizations. Leaders, who have a deep sense of purpose and are true to their core values. We need leaders with the courage to build their companies to meet the needs of all stakeholders, and who recognize the importance of their service to society."*

Corporate responsibility has always been about values and value creation. Yet in an economy where corporate acquisitions and layoffs of tens of thousands of workers are more the norm, and serving the greater good often is a distant second, few CEOs have successfully transformed their strategic thinking or how their organizations do business along the lines that George espouses.…

To achieve these ends, more attention must also be paid to leader education. After all, CEOs of most multinationals were never trained and educated to lead such complex organizations, while still being accountable to multiple stakeholders whose cultural norms may redefine CR as we know it, as well as dictate entirely new expectations.

A review of the core curricula at the top graduate schools in business management, still considered a prerequisite for aspiring corporate leaders, finds some courses, at least, touch on areas that prepare students to think beyond satisfying only shareholders. However, more transformative opportunities in leadership development are still largely the domain of Executive Education programs, whose students are rarely CEOs.

We are not teaching our CEOs, board chairpersons, heads of nonprofit organizations, future members of Congress, and other leaders about significance, even though it is significance that will enable them to lead the way toward transforming us into a more just, fair, ethical, caring, and, yes, economically successful culture. Part of my goal with this book is to stimulate intelligent dialogue and intense introspection about how we're creating our leaders and how we can move from being a "sanction society" focused on the Gross Domestic Product to an "honor society" focused on, perhaps, a "Gross Significance Product" that measures how many lives have been transformed for the better by each of us. Making that happen is a challenge I put to you, dear reader.

The Seven Keys

Now, let's take a look at the Seven Keys to Significant Leadership, one by one, and I think you will see how they fit into this idea of the paradigm shift. Ask yourself, if you are a leader or aspire to lead an organization one day, how many do you possess?

> *Gross Significance Product*: *A measure not of economic activity, but of the level at which society, both on an individual and an organizational level, changed the lives of people for the better over a set period of time.*

Significance Exercise #13: What Kind of Leader Are You?

There are many ways to lead, but I have identified four very common styles of leadership. Which do you practice? You may not know, but this exercise will help you find out.

For each question, circle answer 1, 2, 3, or 4 and give yourself the same number of points. At the end, add up your total to see what your leadership style is: Inspirational, Confrontational, Collaborative, or Darwinian.

Communication You communicate with your subordinates by...	1. ...respecting their time and only communicating what is necessary. 2. ...to-the-point memos. 3. ...encouraging them to ask questions so they're always in the loop. 4. ...expecting them to keep their ears to the ground.
Management Your favorite tool to manage and direct the people below you is...	1. ...incentives and rewards. 2. ...a "going into battle" culture. 3. ...hands-on feedback. 4. ...implied or direct threats to their job security.
Discipline The best way to maintain employee discipline is...	1. ...making sure people love their work. 2. ...attacking problems as soon as they become apparent. 3. ...being immersed the corporate culture so you know what's brewing. 4. ...giving certain people enough rope to hang themselves.
Motivation You prefer to motivate by...	1. ...setting the example. 2. ...demanding everyone's best at all times. 3. ...training and more training. 4. ...allowing some people to fail very publicly from time to time.
Delegation The most effective way to delegate is to...	1. ...help people make your goals their goals, then trust them. 2. ...give clear orders and let people know the consequences for not following them. 3. ...show people how you want it done. 4. ...hire the right people, then get out of the way and let them do their jobs.
Crisis You best manage a crisis by...	1. ...making sure everyone has a stake in the organization's well-being. 2. ...making all the decisions. 3. ...consulting with experts throughout the organization before decisions are made. 4. ...taking care of yourself, as the leader, first.

Scoring

4-8 points: You're an Inspirational leader who leads by exciting others and drawing them into your vision.

10-14 points: You're a Confrontational leader with a no-nonsense, demand-the-best attitude.

15-19 points: You're a Collaborative leader who likes to get his or her hands dirty and work with your people.

20-24 points: You're a Darwinian leader who believes in letting people rise or fall on their own merits.

1. Compassion

N.: A sincere awareness and consciousness of others' distress or misfortune, paired with a desire to alleviate or help to overcome it.

> *A human being is a part of the whole called by us universe, a part limited in time and space. He experiences himself, his thoughts and feelings as something separated from the rest, a kind of optical delusion of his consciousness. This delusion is a kind of prison for us, restricting us to our personal desires and to affection for a few persons nearest to us. Our task must be to free ourselves from this prison by widening our circle of compassion to embrace all living creatures and the whole of nature in its beauty.*
>
> —*Albert Einstein, German theoretical physicist*

You may be familiar with one of Aesop's fables called "The Belly and its Members," which speaks to the importance of contributing to the greater good for the benefit of the whole. The story goes that the members of the "body" become fed up with the wants and needs of the stomach, accusing it of doing nothing but resting and enjoying luxury and self-indulgence, while they do all the work to feed it. The members of the body then boycott the stomach, resolving that they will no longer lend their assistance to the belly. Without the nourishment that was provided when the members were working together, the body quickly becomes weak, and the individual parts—hands, feet, heart, mouth, lungs—cease to function, regretting their oversight only after it's too late. The fable concludes by explaining that, "As in the body, so in the state, each member in his proper sphere must work for the common good."

> *If any film of recent times features a lead character that demonstrates true selflessness, it would be* Hotel Rwanda. *The 2004 historical drama is about the 1994 Rwanda Genocide and is rated among the top one hundred most inspirational movies of all time. The movie's lead character, hotelier Paul Rusesabagina, exemplifies significance, risking his life because of his compassion for all people.*
>
> *The movie portrays the civil war between the Hutu and Tutsi people of Rwanda. As the Hutus carry out brutal genocide against the Tutsi people, Rusesabagina, a Hutu, uses his favor among people of influence to bribe, negotiate, and sometimes outwit officials to keep his family, friends, and neighbors safe, regardless of their ethnic group.*
>
> *Recognizing the evil ensuing around him, he risks his life providing shelter in his hotel to more than twelve hundred Tutsi people, who would otherwise be beaten and killed by the marauding Hutu death squads.*

Significant Leaders are able to see beyond their own desires, troubles, abilities, and deficiencies in order to see what they can do to aid others. A selfless Significant Leader understands that when the people beneath him or her in the hierarchy are assisted in bringing out their full potential and achieving their highest level of personal growth and professional success, everyone benefits, including the leader.

Significant Leaders exhibit selflessness in many forms. To be compassionate, they must be able to put themselves in the shoes of another person and understand the issues and challenges that person is going through. Such empathy is vital to understanding the needs of others. Selflessness also involves awareness and consideration of the consequences one's behavior has on others, no matter how small the action. A selfless leader always considers the fallout from a decision and how it will impact others. Finally, a selfless leader recognizes the worth and humanity in all individuals, regardless of differences or stations in life.

2. Clarity

N: A precise, unambiguous understanding of a situation and the bigger picture around it. Clarity is not just "simplicity," but a more complex perception of the principles, purpose, and path you should take to achieve a goal.

> *More important than the quest for certainty is the quest for clarity.*
> —*Francois Gautier, French journalist and writer*

How often have we seen situations in which a company spends millions of dollars for a mission and vision statement and then seemingly ignores it? The primary reason for this kind of fiasco is that, in order to accomplish a goal, whether it be professional or personal, you must have a clear sense of why you want to accomplish it, what tools and qualities you need and how you and the people around you fit into the plan. Without those basics in place, a mission statement is nothing more than public relations.

All too often, we come up with an idea and a comprehensive plan on paper but are quick to abandon our original intent or overall vision at the first sign of a real challenge or adversity. If you are able to stick to your vision when things get rough, you must have a complete understanding of it and investment in it. You must have clarity: a singular picture of what you want and the process by which you and those under you will get there. If you really know your priorities and your values, it will be easier to avoid abandoning them when you encounter something that is in conflict with your mission.

Clarity also involves an understanding of who else is involved in your mission with you, and how your paths and responsibilities are interconnected. A Significant Leader knows where he or she fits into the picture, but also has a clear view of everyone else's roles, abilities, and agendas and how to put others in a position to succeed. This leader is also clear about what is expected of each person. If the people you lead don't understand what they are trying to accomplish, they will only become confused and frustrated, leaving them unable to carry out the actions necessary to fulfill their individual goals and the larger goal. Each person's action has a consequence, but without the clarity to understand how all of these elements are connected, there can be no accountability. Without accountability, there is only blame and finger-pointing.

> *In his books on leadership, former General Electric CEO Jack Welch explains how clarity can inspire others to act. As a leader, if you can provide a clear vision of how you believe things can be done better, and you are able to articulate the importance of every person's responsibility in making that change happen, people will be inspired to achieve that vision. Great leaders don't have to provide specific direction for how to accomplish a goal as long as there is a shared clarity of everybody's role.*

Clarity is more a way of life than a state of mind. In order to have clarity, you must first acknowledge and care for your own belief system. Often referred to as the "mind's eye," clarity is what helps us visualize our most cherished objectives, whether they be professional or personal. If you understand your values and the driving factors behind them, it is much easier to put them into practice when the time comes to make big decisions. Without clarity—without knowing the "why" as well as the "what"—it can be easy to lose sight of what we want in the first place.

3. Composure

N: The ability to remain calm in mind, emotions, and appearance, regardless of the circumstances.

> *Nothing gives one person so much advantage over another as to remain always cool and unruffled under all circumstances.*
>
> —*Thomas Jefferson, third U.S. president*

To demonstrate how composure can help you keep your mind clear and enhance your ability to serve as an effective leader, think about the process of packing for a trip. Should you ball up your shirts and pants and throw them haphazardly into the suitcase? Or should you fold and arrange each item in the bag so you can maximize your usable space? We should think of the suitcase as our mind, and realize that the more unresolved, out-of-control thoughts, expectations, and issues we allow to clog up our heads, the less room we have for organized and intelligent reflection.

The clear mind afforded by a composed attitude can often save us stress and embarrassment in all aspects of our lives, personal and professional. Even if, on occasion, your mind is racing or your anger is elevating, composure helps you to recognize the comparative triviality of the issue at hand and to harness your passions.

There are exercises we can engage in to ensure composure when it counts … and I'm not just talking about the old "count to ten" trick. Try taking ten minutes for yourself. Retreat after a stressful situation and allow yourself a little introspection. Keep yourself in good health with a good diet and exercise. Whatever it takes, don't let that "suitcase" get too full. Letting your mind unwind, keeping that suitcase clear, will allow you to stay focused and calm when that storm or crisis does arise.

4. Conviction

N: The strength, clarity, and commitment, in mind and actions, to remain dedicated to what you believe in even if you are unsure of the outcome or are facing criticism or opposition.

> *Never doubt that a small group of thoughtful, committed citizens can change the world. Indeed, it's the only thing that ever has.*
> —*Margaret Meade, American cultural anthropologist*

Conviction is the anchor that helps us have clarity and purpose in life. When we read of the feats accomplished by great leaders in history, they are the result of the leaders' convictions and the commitment resulting from those convictions. One such example was William Wilberforce. Born in 1759, Wilberforce became passionate about working toward the abolition of slavery in England. As a member of Parliament from 1780 until 1825, he was tireless in his efforts. Wilberforce had to step down from Parliament due to failing health, but continued his fight. In 1833, the Slavery Abolition Act was passed, outlawing slavery in most of the British Empire. Three days later, Wilberforce died. His entire life was built on the conviction that he must see the end of slavery.

Significance Story

The Boston College Center for Corporate Citizenship and Reputation Institute releases a ranking of dominant, highly recognized companies in the United States based on the public's perception of their "corporate social responsibility," or CSR.

CSR is a concept that involves companies taking responsibility for all of their activities and considering the effects they have on all stakeholders, not just customers. It's a voluntary movement, with organizations taking steps to go beyond their daily business to improve the quality of life for employees and their families as well as for the local community and society at large.

According to the institute, corporate citizenship, governance, and workplace practices account for more than 40 percent of a company's status, which makes it critical for organizations to let the public know how they support good causes, protect the environment, treat their employees, and run their business ethically. Why is CSR in this book? Well, carrying through with programs that yield truly significant results requires significant leadership. A company must first have a clear vision and thorough understanding of its values and principles before it can accomplish anything of significance.

In 2008, these companies were among the top ten in the rankings, carrying the best reputations in the eyes of the public:

1. *Google*
2. *Campbell Soup Co.*
3. *Johnson & Johnson*
4. *Walt Disney Corp.*
5. *Kraft Foods, Inc.*
6. *General Mills*
7. *Levi Strauss & Co.*
8. *UPS*
9. *Berkshire Hathaway*
10. *Microsoft*

Conviction is what draws you to a cause larger than yourself. It drives people to achieve life-changing, history-changing results. It takes a combination of other qualities to really live by your convictions: clarity of beliefs, strong passion (considering that standing up for one's convictions can often mean confronting hostile points of view), confidence, and self-esteem. Great leaders trust their ability to make good, honorable decisions based on their values, even if they don't necessary have the "right" answer in a given situation. As a leader, you must embody these qualities in order to live by your convictions so you can effect positive change when your values deem it necessary.

5. Character

N: The traits, qualities, and characteristics that demonstrate who you are as an individual.

The best index to a person's character is (a) how he treats people who can't do him any good, and (b) how he treats people who can't fight back.

—*Abigail Van Buren, American advice columnist*

When thinking about how character works and how it is at the very core of how you are perceived as a leader, it can be helpful to think of a character in a book. Think about the last novel you read. How did you come to develop feelings about the characters? How did you determine who was the antagonist or protagonist of the story? It is simple: You judged those characters on their *character*. You used their actions and behaviors to determine whether they were a good or a bad force. Those who were honorable and just were heroes, while those who were deceitful and hurtful to others were villains. It's the same in life.

Think back to our comparison of faiths for a moment. Remember the Confucian belief that a person should be judged on moral fiber and respectable behavior? Bear this in mind when reflecting on your character. What defines you? Is it where your parents came from, what you do and how much money you make? Or would you rather be known for whether you stand on your principles, whether you do what you promise, and how you influence the people around you? A Significant Leader would opt for the second set of defining characteristics, as these are the only ones that will fuel your legacy.

When considering your own character, think about a child in school as he or she reads history books about great leaders of the past. The child has never met these people, heard them speak, or actually witnessed them doing a good deed, but these people's actions and attributes live on beyond the pages to form their character. Remember, when we strip away titles, degrees, and even names, a person's character stands upon only one thing: Is he or she as good as his or her word? It is your decisions and your honor that will build your character and determine how your life would look in the pages of a history book.

6. Confidence

N: The self-assurance and certitude in one's own power and ability.

The man who has confidence in himself gains the confidence of others.

—*Hasidic saying*

I have a friend who, very early in her career, landed a job at a major advertising agency. While extremely intelligent and innovative, she was young at the time and intimidated by some of the older, more experienced account handlers she was working alongside. She told me once of a brainstorming session for a new client, where everyone, including her veteran counterparts, was at a creative loss for an innovative approach to a client's advertising campaign. Suddenly, my friend had a stroke of genius. But while she was eager to share her idea, she was afraid to speak up, worried her inspiration might not match up to the expectations of her managers. A moment later, her account supervisor, more than fifteen years her senior in the industry, exclaimed that he'd come up with a phenomenal concept, and proceeded to explain his vision for a campaign, which ended up being extremely similar to the idea my friend had come up with. The campaign was a great success.

Though she experienced a brief bout of regret about her hesitation to speak out, my friend learned a life lesson that day. Always be confident in your abilities, even in the face of adversity or when it appears your ideas might not be up to par with the expectations of other people. If you don't have the confidence to act, you'll never know what outcome may have occurred.

A discussion on confidence demands one important side note: Confidence is not the same as *arrogance*. The Significant Leader, while confident, is conscious of and open to other opinions or options. Significant Leaders recognize and admit when they make mistakes, instead of covering them up or blaming others, because their innate confidence is not threatened by the fact that they are capable of mistakes like anyone else. In fact, the Significant Leader uses failure as an opportunity to learn.

Just as we discussed in previous chapters, an excess of anything can be bad; moderation is key. So it is with confidence. *Over*confidence can cause a leader to become entrapped in his or her ego, ignoring the opinions and needs of others, ostracizing employees, friends, or family, and often turning to corruption. Self-assuredness paired with awareness, not self-importance, is what gives rise to significance.

7. Courage

N: The mental state that enables one to face fear or adversity without faltering in what one needs to do.

> *Without courage, wisdom bears no fruit.*
> —*Baltasar Gracian, seventeenth century Spanish writer and Jesuit educator*

This is the most important of the leadership qualities we discuss. It will dictate your ability to step up and do the right thing when called upon. When you think about it, true courage, the type that contributes to significance, can be boiled down to a simple formula:

Honorable Intent + Action = Courage

The key concept here is the "intent." Let's consider for, example, one group of people that is often admired and considered to be "courageous": professional athletes. While there is generally no harm in appreciating a famous football hero, I would argue that famous athletes don't embody true courage. Sheer strength, commendable skill, and passion for their profession, sure, but the intent of these athletes is based more on financial return, competition, and entertainment than on filling a true human need. Courage doesn't always come along with fame, fortune, or recognition.

Genuine courage emerges when a person faces odds that make what he or she wants to achieve seem hazardous or impossible, and persists anyway. Think Lance Armstrong, defying cancer to win the Tour de France, or Christopher Reeve moving past his horrible accident to become a spokesman for spinal cord injuries, then to act and direct again. Personally, when I think of courage, the image that often comes to me is of the blood donor who overcomes a fear of needles in order to give blood because he or she knows it is the right thing to do.

The importance of courage for you, as a Significant Leader, becomes obvious when you consider the intellectual outcasts and daring entrepreneurs who have endured great hardship to make humanity better. Just imagine if Copernicus had not stood steadfast to defend his theory that the earth was not the "center of the universe." Imagine if Martin Luther King had not stood up against discrimination, stepping out from behind the comfort of his Sunday pulpit to challenge the evil of racism. What if the suffragettes had remained silent instead of fighting for women's rights? We would not have seen the historic year of female presidential and vice presidential candidates in 2008. You, like these "heroes" of the past, have the ability to inspire and encourage people if you, too, act according to your beliefs.

Remember that not every courageous act is accompanied by an outcome fit for history books. Significant Leaders need only to display courage by having the mental strength, confidence, and honorable intent to make decisions that contribute to the best interest of not just themselves, but the whole. Courage often means defying convention, going against common wisdom and earning the enmity of many people. But as I've said before, take this as a sign you're doing something right. Courageous acts are the ultimate acts of true leadership.

Significance Exercise #14: The Seven C's

This exercise should look familiar. You're going to ask three people who know you well to rate you for each of the Seven C's of Significant Leadership. But two new wrinkles: You're going to do it anonymously and you're going to rate yourself as well, then compare your score with the average of the other three.

Ask three colleagues or close subordinates who know your work very well to rate you on the Seven C's using a scale of one to ten, with ten being the most favorable. Make the replies anonymous so there's no worry about professional consequences. Rate yourself in the appropriate box as well. Use the descriptions of each of the Seven C's below.

Compassion The ability to act selflessly to aid another	**Clarity** Precise, unambiguous understanding of a situation	**Composure** The ability to look, seem and be calm under all circumstances
Your self-rating: **First person's rating:** **Second person's rating:** **Third person's rating:** **Average of the three:** _____	**Your self-rating:** **First person's rating:** **Second person's rating:** **Third person's rating:** **Average of the three:** _____	**Your self-rating:** **First person's rating:** **Second person's rating:** **Third person's rating:** **Average of the three:** _____
Conviction Acting according to principles from which you never deviate	**Character** Being defined by inner qualities such as honesty, strength and commitment	**Confidence** Self-assurance in your own abilities
Your self-rating: **First person's rating:** **Second person's rating:** **Third person's rating:** **Average of the three:** _____	**Your self-rating:** **First person's rating:** **Second person's rating:** **Third person's rating:** **Average of the three:** _____	**Your self-rating:** **First person's rating:** **Second person's rating:** **Third person's rating:** **Average of the three:** _____
Courage The fortitude to stay the right course in the face of pressure	**Scoring (your average for each C)**	
Your self-rating: **First person's rating:** **Second person's rating:** **Third person's rating:** **Average of the three:** _____	8-10: This is a foundational aspect of your leadership. 5-7: This C could be stronger in order to make you a more significant leader. 1-4: This is actually harming your ability to lead others into significance. Improving in this area should be a top priority. **How did you rate yourself versus the other three? Did you score higher or lower in each area? What does that mean for your self-assessment of your leadership ability?**	

Next Steps for Significance Seekers...

- *... Reflect on a time when one of your people needed compassion. What did you do and what could you have done differently?*

- *... How clear is your vision for your organization? Can you write it in no more than fifteen words? Try and keep trying.*

- *... Find a "fetish object" like a coin or carving you can keep in your pocket. The next time a situation that requires composure comes up and you're tempted to lose your self-control, feel the object and use it to anchor yourself in a calm, rational state of mind. How does this change your actions?*

- *... What single conviction most strongly drives your leadership of your organization?*

- *... Write down the names of ten people, living or dead, who exemplify qualities of character you would like to manifest.*

- *... What three actions could you take now that would bolster the confidence of the people working under you?*

- *... What courageous decision could your organization make that would transform it for the better? What would be the risks?*

CHAPTER NINE
The Seven Faces of a Significant Manager

QUALITIES THAT CAN BRING A MIDLEVEL MANAGER TO AN EXCEPTIONAL LEVEL OF SIGNIFICANCE ... AND PERHAPS SET THE STAGE FOR FUTURE LEADERSHIP

Management is nothing more than motivating other people.
—Lee Iacocca, former president and CEO of Chrysler Corp.

A Significant Manager is a Significant Leader in microcosm. That is, he or she fills the same role as a CEO or company president, just on a smaller scale and with the additional challenge of dealing with the needs of people up the chain of command. But while the basic philosophy is similar, managers face their own obstacles and opportunities. And since there are far more corporate managers than C-level leaders, they wield great influence over the shaping of lives and careers. So let's ask, what a Significant Manager?

A Significant Manager is involved with his or her employees and understands that work is about them, not him or her. Significant Managers have come to understand that, in their role, they are most successful when they learn to get work done through others, to motivate employees to achieve organizational goals by helping them achieve their personal goals in the process. Just as overall significance means acting in ways that bring hope and promise to others as well as yourself, the core idea behind significant management is that if you can inspire and assist the people you manage to fulfill their potential through their work, you will enable to them to achieve their best possible job performance, thereby improving the organization. It's "Be all you can be" transformed into "Be all *we* can be."

There are many ways a Significant Manager can do this:

- Showing respect for the employee.
- Fostering pride in accomplishments and giving credit where credit is due.
- Encouraging employees to share their ideas and bring their own talents to a project.
- Showing loyalty.
- Asking employees to collaborate with you.

The Bar is Set Low

The Significant Manager is willing to help others pursue their own significance and develop along with the company. Unfortunately, this attitude, both at a personal and a corporate level, is harder to find these days. Fifty years ago, you signed on to work for a company and you stayed there through retirement. You were part of the family. Now, thanks to technology, outsourcing, and market pressures, as well as a restlessly entrepreneurial culture, companies don't keep people for decades. They downsize. They export jobs. The idea has become "Don't get too close; that way you won't feel bad when you have to lay them off." There is far less loyalty, and so there are fewer managers who feel they have a substantial investment in the futures of their employees. The bar has dropped low indeed for managers caring about those they manage.

As a Significant Manager, it's your job to defy that trend. There was never anything flawed about the idea of helping foster greater personal responsibility and achievement among employees; it simply went out of fashion. But it's a powerful tool; it can even become a competitive advantage. How would your organization benefit if you could garner the employee loyalty and passion of a company like clothing maker Patagonia or Internet giant Google, which treat people like family, give them room to express their ideas, and reward them commensurate with their results? Would helping your people become significant transform your organization into a market leader?

When they are faced with making decisions amid corporate politics, or when they are approaching a crossroads in their career, Significant Managers examine their beliefs and use their value systems to make decisions, knowing they may be inviting criticism from peers and leaders. They will take the risk to make the right versus the popular decision for themselves and for the people under them. Significant Managers do not take credit for their team's success. They *give* credit and are more interested in promoting the skills and talents of the people they lead, giving recognition and appreciation when and where it is due. They know that in the long run, if they empower and recognize the people who make their performance possible, everyone will benefit. Great managers are those who make the people below them better and stronger. In other words, they grow the people who could ultimately replace them.

> *A good manager is a man who isn't worried about his own career but rather the careers of those who work for him.*
>
> —*H.S.M. Burns, former president of Shell Oil*

Theory X and Theory Y

Consider the concepts of "Theory X" and "Theory Y" proposed by Douglas M. McGregor, former professor at the Sloan School of Management at Massachusetts Institute of Technology. "Theory X" presents the conventional view shared by most managers:

1. Management is solely responsible for elements of productive enterprise—money, materials, equipment, people—and delivering on the economic and productive needs of the organization.
2. Managers must direct the efforts of people—motivating them, controlling their actions, and modifying their behaviors to fit the needs of the organization.
3. People are passive and resistant to organizational needs. Therefore, they must be persuaded, rewarded, punished, and controlled by managers. This is the managers' task.
4. By nature, the average worker is indolent—working as little as possible.
5. The average worker lacks ambition, avoids responsibility, and prefers to be directed or led.
6. He is gullible and not very smart and can easily be duped.

That's more than just wrongheaded, it's offensive. It assumes that the worker is going to do as little as possible and take as much as possible, in effect defrauding the company. How would you expect your employees to feel if they came to a workplace where they were regarded with such suspicion and contempt?

In contrast, "Theory Y" takes a different view of human nature and human motivation:

1. Management is responsible for *organizing* the elements of productive enterprise—money, materials, equipment, people—in the *interest* of economic ends.

2. People are *not* by nature resistant to the needs of the organization. If apathy is prevalent among the front-line employees, it has been created by the managers, leaders, and culture of the organization.

3. It is management's responsibility to make it possible for people to develop the characteristics that help them deliver on the needs of the organization. The motivation, potential for development, capacity for assuming responsibility, and ability to direct behavior toward achieving organizational goals *is present in people.*

4. The primary task of managers is to create or arrange organizational conditions, processes, and methods of operation so people can achieve their personal *best* by directing *their own* efforts toward organizational objectives.

Significance Exercise #15: Your Theory

You've seen Theory X and Theory Y. What is your theory about managing others? Even if you're not a manager, you must have some ideas about how you would manage other people if put in that position. Time to share them with the class.

In the first section, write down up to five principles that inform your management style. In the second section, write down the five principles that guided the most memorable (best or worst) manager you ever had.

Your own management theory:

1.

2.

3.

4.

5.

The theory of your most memorable manager:

1.

2.

3.

4.

5.

"Theory Y" accurately represents the characteristics and attributes of a Significant Manager, presenting a management philosophy that is based primarily on creating opportunities, releasing potential, removing obstacles, encouraging growth, and providing guidance.

Seven Managerial Faces

As you will see, to bring his or her personal theory into practice, the Significant Manager puts into action the same seven attributes as the Significant Leader. The difference lies in how they are applied. Significant Leaders approach these seven attributes from a higher, more strategic plane. The Significant Manager, however, must demonstrate these attributes in a more tactical, hands-on, interactive approach, with employees, peers, and partners achieving success for the organization. Each attribute represents a different "face" employees see, and they will respond and perform based on how that face makes them feel—respected and appreciated or doubted and used.

Because I defined them in Chapter Eight, I'll bypass definitions and move directly into a discussion of how each of these vital qualities marks the Significant Manager.

1. **Compassion**

    Like a Significant Leader, a Significant Manager demonstrates compassion for the employees who are crucial in getting work done. The Significant Manager is willing to take the risk and sacrifice short-term efficiencies in order to meet the needs of the employees. He or she is looking beyond the current moment, projecting to the long-term success that will be delivered by employees when they feel valued and respected as individuals.

    In this context, compassion involves knowing and understanding the day-to-day challenges faced by each employee, which could range from medical issues to childcare to a stressful financial situation. Only when the manager grasps the nature of each person's life can he or she show the proper "applied compassion" by making an effort to shape the working environment and duties to make dealing with the other aspects of the person's life easier. Likewise, when the Significant Manager understands the employee's goals and dreams, he or she can apply compassion in a way that furthers those goals and dreams, earning strong loyalty from each subordinate.

    A young woman at a large corporation had worked very hard to achieve success. Five years earlier, she had received her first promotion and throughout her career had given unconditionally to the needs of the company. She worked sixty to eighty hours per week, often on the night shift, despite the fact that she had a young child. But when she and her husband celebrated the birth of their second child, she suddenly realized she could not and did not desire to continue in that role; she wanted to spend more time with her children. She had missed many important events in the life of her first child while she pursued success at any cost and was not willing to maintain that level of personal sacrifice.

> **Applied compassion:** *Knowing and appreciating a person's circumstances so you can help that individual further his or her goals in a practical way.*

In a panic, she called the manager who had been holding her position while she was on maternity leave. Sobbing and apologizing, she told him she could not come back to that job. Her children had replaced her career as the most important thing in her life. The guilt was overwhelming because she knew her manager had made a great sacrifice in holding her position, which required his managing a very busy operation short-staffed, and that he was dependent on her return.

Rather than act as though she were letting him down, or becoming angry and accusatory, her manager was empathetic and compassionate. He told her not to worry; it would all work out. He immediately placed her in a clerical position that had just become available and did not once question her capabilities or aptitude for the new job. By showing trust and compassion, he provided her with an environment that fit the needs of her family and rewarded her for her years of dedication and hard work in her previous role—and enabled the company to retain one of its most dedicated people.

This manager understood that the short-term pain of being short-staffed was worth helping a loyal and hard-working employee, which resulted in her staying with the organization and creating long-term benefits for the company. She became one of the company's most satisfied, loyal people, a true human resource.

Significant Managers think of their people as individuals *first*, with personal needs and wants that will often come before their job. It is the task of this sort of manager to enable employees to blend their personal and professional lives so that one serves the other and they genuinely feel that "The company cares about me."

Significance Story

One winter night, an old couple dashed into the lobby of a small Philadelphia hotel, hoping for a room. But the clerk said, "All the rooms are full." As they started to leave, he said, "Would you be willing to sleep in my room? It's not a suite, but I think you'll be comfortable."

At first they were reluctant, but he insisted, "Don't worry; I can sleep in the office." So they accepted. The next morning, when it was time to check out, the old gentleman said to the clerk, "Thank you; you should be the manager of the best hotel in the country. Maybe someday I'll build one for you." Amused, the clerk smiled and thanked him.

Two years later, the clerk received a round-trip ticket to New York City and a letter thanking him for his kindness. The old couple was inviting him to come and visit them. Although he'd forgotten the incident, he decided to accept the offer. When he arrived in New York City, they took him to the corner of Thirty-fourth Street and Fifth Avenue. "That," said the old gentleman, pointing to a magnificent skyscraper, "is the hotel that I have just built for you to manage."

The clerk said, "You must be joking."

"I can assure you I'm not," the man said.

The old gentleman's name was William Waldorf Astor. The hotel was the original Waldorf-Astoria. The young clerk was George C. Bolt, its first manager.

2. Clarity

Significant Managers who demonstrate clarity not only understand the organization's vision and mission, but have a clear understanding of how their department delivers on that vision and mission. They are able to communicate the message, vision, or mission to their employees in such a way that the employees are motivated and inspired to serve the goals of the organization. The employees understand the role they play as important individuals in achieving worthwhile goals.

Managers with clarity demonstrate three critical success factors:

1. A deep understanding of the organization's long-term strategy.
2. A clear understanding of how their department synergistically interacts with other departments to serve that strategy.

3. The awareness that their competency in communicating the strategy, mission, methods, and rewards to people working under them will determine how successfully they are able to deliver.

Significant Managers have the ability to look up from the day-to-day grind and see the big picture, how they and their team fit into the organization's broader goals and future. They also realize it is critical to ensure all employees understand their common purpose in the same way. At Walt Disney World, one of the manager's primary roles is to ensure that the employees—or Cast Members, as the company calls them—understand their true purpose, no matter the job or task they were hired to perform. Everyone at Walt Disney World is part of the mission known as "Creating Happiness." So whether their job is to serve food in a restaurant or sweep the streets, Cast Members understand their task is an important part of a larger mission. Part of Disney managers' duty is to consistently remind Cast Members of this fact—to inspire them by letting them know they are part of something bigger and greater than themselves.

Significant Managers are also clear communicators. They take the time to communicate expectations, the rewards and consequences for behaviors, the reasons behind decisions, and the processes that determine the policies which affect their daily lives. It is their job to ensure employees are informed, not ignorant, so they can carry out their duties and produce both personal gratification and success for the organization. They create and perpetuate an environment of success by validating and rewarding good performance, holding people accountable for poor behavior or lack of productivity, and removing roadblocks and obstacles.

The Significant Manager also regards his or her personal values and core beliefs with clarity. It is difficult to lead if you don't know what you stand for. By articulating these guiding principles, a manager achieves significance by living his or her values and beliefs. We will discuss this later in more detail as it relates to the other attributes. As Walt Disney's brother and business collaborator Roy Disney once said, "It's easy to make decisions once you know what your values are."

3. Composure

Managers must realize that dealing with crisis is a critical part of their job description. It's not a matter of *if* a crisis will occur, just *when*. Employees will make mistakes, markets will tumble, disasters will happen. One of the key qualities that distinguishes a Significant Manager from other managers is how that person prepares for and respond to crises and emergencies.

Managers must always keep in mind that their reaction to a difficult period reveals much about them. As the saying goes, "Adversity doesn't build character, it reveals it." By responding to a crisis with panic, blaming, or anger, you will be giving everyone who works with you a negative impression of your character—and, unfortunately, a clear insight into your true nature that may make it impossible for you to effectively govern your department in the future. In the end, you lose the respect of your employees, peers, business partners, and customers. You could lose business or have people transfer from your supervision because they can no longer work for you. Such a situation could even turn you into a liability, costing you your job.

In the same way, a positive response in a crisis can enhance your personal brand and your leadership ability. Composure means anticipating possible problems and having plans in place to deal with them, and when difficulties arise, addressing them with a cool head, a clear grasp of the chain of command, the ability to delegate, and a strong sense of personal responsibility. Talk is cheap. If you comport yourself with professionalism, grace, and composure during hard times, you will not only advance your career and earn the respect of those with whom you work, but you will also burnish and deepen your own character, transforming who you see when you look in the mirror.

We hope, as a people and as a nation, that we never again have to experience an event like the terrorist attacks of September 11, 2001. On this terrifying and heartbreaking day, we witnessed the strengths and heroism of many men and women who maintained their composure under the most unfathomable circumstances. They were and are truly significant individuals under fire.

My friend Mary worked for the Disney Institute at Walt Disney World. She was a Business Program Facilitator, and on September 11 she and a colleague were co-facilitating a business program for an international group of executives. The program was a three-day "Disney's Approach to Loyalty" program, and they were in the first full day of classroom content and activities.

During the break, a Disney Institute manager entered the room and told the two facilitators about the plane flying into the first tower of the World Trade Center. At this point, no one suspected terrorism, believing only that it was a terrible accident. The facilitators were asked to make an announcement to the group to keep them informed of the breaking news. After making the announcement, the group was scheduled to embark on a field trip to Disney's Grand Floridian Hotel and Resort, where they would participate in several activities and have lunch. Everyone loaded onto the bus for the short ride to the hotel. The bus driver had turned on the small television at the front of the bus and everyone watched in horror as the first tower collapsed. Shortly after arriving at the hotel, the facilitators found out there had also been an attack on the second tower and it had collapsed, too.

As you can imagine, the shock and grief were palpable. The facilitators asked if there were members in the group who needed to leave to make phone calls or return to their businesses. Two participants whose corporate headquarters were located in one of the twin towers expressed an urgency to get back as soon as possible. The facilitators made the appropriate arrangements.

The remaining participants were then given the option of continuing with the program for the next two days or canceling with a full refund. Surprisingly, all of the remaining participants wanted to continue. My friend told me she and her colleague considered these the toughest three days of their lives. As a professional representing the Disney organization, a company recognized for its unprecedented service to guests, it was imperative that they set their emotions aside and deliver the quality, caring service for which Disney is known. They cried at home every night, but during the program, they not only maintained their composure, they demonstrated the appropriate level of professionalism and ensured a positive experience for all of the guests.

Significant Managers know that when they are stressed for reasons of professional or personal conflict, it is unacceptable to take it out on their employees, peers, partners, or customers. They realize the importance of maintaining composure during tense situations and presenting a cool, professional, and composed exterior to everyone around them. Significant Managers hold their temper, measure their responses, control their emotions … and have a strong, loving personal environment where they can allow their feelings free rein, so they can return to work with composure.

4. Conviction

Managers who demonstrate significance often find themselves challenging the status quo or current policies and processes. They are innovative thinkers, sure in their convictions and willing to present new ideas, even if it means contradicting the popular opinions and ideas of peers, leaders, or industry standards.

They do not accept "We've always done it this way" as an explanation, and don't remain silent in the face of practices that contradict the way things should be done. They agree with the classic definition of insanity: "Doing the same thing over and over in the same way and expecting different results." They live by the belief that employees have great ideas and they can be motivated and inspired to deliver exceptional results to the organization. Here's what I mean:

Debbie, a young restaurant manager, is in charge of a pizza restaurant that is a significant source of revenue for her company. On one occasion, she arrives at the pizza stand to find that the employees have done an excellent job of preparing for the day's business, and she notes that customers are already beginning to line up for lunch.

When she walks to the kitchen, however, she notices a sour smell. On further inspection, it seems to be coming from the oven, where the first batch of fresh pizzas is falling off the chain onto the table for cutting. The smell intensifies. She calls her front-line leader to the kitchen, and he validates that the smell is coming from the cooked pizzas. She quickly makes the decision to shut down the restaurant and delay the delivery of food, apologizing to the customers. This announcement makes several customers angry and they vow to file complaints.

Looking for the source of the problem, Debbie pulls all of the frozen pizzas from the holding cooler and checks the expiration dates. Surprisingly, all of the dates show the inventory to be good for three more days. Puzzled, but not willing to risk making customers ill, she tests several more pizzas by cooking them in the chain-driven oven. As before, under heat, the pizzas smell sour.

At this point she has reached a crossroads. She can cook the pizzas and serve them to the customers, knowing she be will protected by the dates on the boxes though she will risk making customers ill, or keep the location closed until safe pizzas can be acquired, understanding that the loss of revenue for the day will be significant. She will possibly experience a reprimand from her superior as well as a loss of business.

Ultimately, Debbie decides to keep the location closed, making arrangements for replacement pizzas. This decision is based on her personal values and her conviction that she is doing the right thing. She is willing to face the consequences for her decision because of her strong belief that her reasons are sound. However, when her district manager finds out, he is furious and demands that she open the store immediately.

Debbie now finds herself at a second crossroads: Do as she is told and defy her convictions, or refuse and risk termination. Again, her values win out. She informs her boss that she cannot, in good conscience, cook and serve the pizzas to the customers, risking their health and possible legal action against the company. He backs down and the stand remains closed until the replacement pizzas arrive, opening late and missing the lucrative lunch rush. Further investigation reveals that maintenance employees had shut down the cooler for six hours while making repairs, resulting in the spoiling of the pizzas. Debbie had saved the company from embarrassment and possible legal action because she'd stood by her convictions.

Holding to personal convictions can be difficult, especially in the face of peer or superior pressure. But Significant Managers know that when they do what is right, they will always be rewarded.

This piece from *U.S. News and World Report* is a wonderful example of putting your money and time where your convictions are:

In the midst of the subprime mortgage crisis, most bankers are fleeing from at-risk homeowners. But a bank in south Chicago is running toward them with open arms. ShoreBank is courting low-income homeowners threatened by exploding adjustable-rate mortgages and persuading them to refinance with stable fixed-rate mortgages. Since September, the bank has closed on twenty-six loans worth $4.5 million—with more to come.

The program is typical of ShoreBank, which devotes itself to investing in neighborhoods that many bankers wouldn't dare enter, professionally or personally. In south Chicago alone, this little economic engine-that-could has invested nearly three billion dollars financing, among other things, 52,000 affordable housing units. And ShoreBank did it all while exceeding performances of some larger, traditional banks. Today ShoreBank Corp. operates in five states and is worth $2.1 billion, officially making it a big player, albeit, one fixed on helping the little guy.

Continued ➤

Community activists by night and bankers by day, Ron Grzywinski, Milton Davis, James Fletcher, and Mary Houghton founded ShoreBank in 1973 as a reaction to the civil rights movement and President Johnson's big-government Great Society. A better fix, they reasoned, would be to give minorities access to capital. At the time, banks routinely denied loans to minorities, a practice called redlining. The founders' idea was based on a risky proposition: "What if your core business had some purpose other than making money?" says Houghton, now president of ShoreBank Corp.

With a $2.4 million loan, they bought their own bank in the South Shore, a community plagued by white flight and urban decay. Their colleagues thought they were crazy. "There was a general bias in dealing with minorities," says Grzywinski, a Chicago native and chairman of ShoreBank, "and a bias that this was the role of the government, not the private sector." The plan to spur small business largely failed, for the usual reasons: intense competition from suburban chain stores and malls. While ShoreBank managed to develop a nearby shopping center that provides the community's only supermarket and financed the purchase of single-family homes, it found its real niche in an unlikely place—rental housing.

Houghton, sixty-six, and Grzywinski, seventy-one (Fletcher and Davis have died), call the secret to their success "Ma and Pa rehabbers"—regular folks willing to take a gamble on fixing up and renting out neighborhood buildings. By focusing on south Chicago, ShoreBank saw each loan and rehabilitated building reinforce the value of its surroundings. In the beginning, the bank required rehabbers to live on site, avoiding the plague of absentee landlords. The bank also encouraged external renovations noticeable to passersby to boost morale. "If a bank disinvests in a community, it meant the neighborhood was going down," Grzywinski says. "We believed the opposite was true."

Grzywinski took his fight to Congress, where he was the sole banker to testify in support of the Community Reinvestment Act, which banned redlining in 1977. ShoreBank has also advised Muhammad Yunus, the Nobel Prize-winning founder of Grameen Bank, which launched the microcredit movement in India.

The bank even inspired then-Gov. Bill Clinton, who launched the similar Southern Development Bancorporation in Arkansas in 1988. As president, Clinton established the Community Development Financial Institutions Fund, which supports more than fifty community development banks and funds. "All these investments," Clinton told U.S News, *"were inspired by the ShoreBank model and the leadership of Ron Grzywinski and Mary Houghton."*

Today, ShoreBank has added environmental impacts to its mission, offering free energy audits of homes and pushing energy efficiency improvements with home loans. The bank has expanded to Cleveland, Detroit, and the Pacific Northwest, while ShoreBank International has taken its ideas overseas. From her desk in the original branch in South Shore, Houghton nevertheless considers the bank's investment here "the single most important thing we've ever done. It's a nice neighborhood now."

5. Character

Conviction is *establishing* what is important to you; character is *living* what is important to you. Significant Managers demonstrate conviction by taking the time to identify their personal values and core beliefs and demonstrate character by living those values and beliefs in their daily activities. You are what you do; words mean less than actions. If your employees were asked to identify your values, would they know them based on your behavior? So, if you say family or balance is important to you, are you making those tough decisions to attend your son's game or be with your family when they need you? You are fooling yourself if you think your employees are not watching all that you do, looking for alignment with your stated values and your behavior.

We've talked about authenticity as one of the Seven Keys. Authenticity is a quality of true character, meaning that you live by what is important to you whether anyone is around to see or not. Are you the same person all the time or do you exhibit Jekyll and Hyde characteristics? Are you calm and professional when things are going well and angry and abusive when times are stressful? Are you ethical when the boss is watching, only to cheat or gossip as soon as his or her back is turned? Character means being consistent with your personal values and actions in all situations.

Significant Managers who demonstrate strong character do not ask employees, peers, or partners to do anything they are not willing to do themselves. Many premier organizations require managers to assume an entry-level position for one day at least once a year in order for them to develop perspective. The Walt Disney Company, Continental Airlines, and Amazon. com are among a few that do this. Loews Hotels Chief Executive Jonathan Tisch spent a day working as a bellman and a housekeeper. After perspiring in his uniform, he ordered the style and material of the uniforms altered to provide comfort for the front-line workers. Carolyn Kibler, Vice President of DaVita Inc. dialysis clinics, became more lenient with administrative delays that were caused by staffing shortages after spending three days on the floor taking care of dialysis patients. Kibler says the physical demands on workers and their capacity for compassion prompted her to reform some administrative procedures for clinics in order to reduce stress on staff.

Try this experiment in your department or organization: Suggest that each executive and manager spend a day working in a front-line job. You will know by their reactions which managers are on the road to significance. They will be the ones who react positively, seeing it as a learning experience and a chance to build relationships with employees.

Significant Managers also demonstrate character by building relationships and trust with employees, peers, and partners. They do this by following through on what they say they will do and demonstrating integrity in their behaviors and actions. They do not prejudge, and they believe the best of people. They take personal responsibility for their actions, learning from their mistakes and willingly sharing those lessons with others to create a learning culture. They do not take credit solely for themselves but instead recognize their teams, without whom they would achieve little.

Warren Bennis says it best in his article in *The Costco Connection* from March 2004, "Leadership is Based on Character":

> *At the end of the day, character is the core competency of leadership. Everything else is perishable. This brings me to another tripod, that of character, and this one must be kept in balance or it tips over: (1) ambition and drive; (2) competence and expertise; and (3) a well-exercised moral compass. An effective leader balances these forces. Drive without competence and integrity produces a demagogue. Competence without integrity and drive manifests a technocrat. Someone who has ambition and competence but is void of integrity is a destructive achiever.*
>
> *Leadership is both sun and soil; it simultaneously empowers one to achieve and feeds the spirit. That is perhaps all we really need to understand.*

> *Weakness of attitude becomes weakness of character.*
> —Albert Einstein, German theoretical physicist

---

6. Confidence

Significant Managers have confidence in their abilities, and when given a new task or project, they do not think about failure. They know how to use their resources and mobilize people to accomplish a task. They believe in their abilities and the abilities of their employees. They do not micromanage; they trust their employees and are secure in giving them the tools, knowledge, skills, and support to enable them to be successful. Although they are confident in their own abilities, they are not afraid or unwilling to ask for help or advice from leaders, mentors, peers, partners, and even employees. Perhaps most importantly, they trust the decisions they have made to hire, promote, or assign work, knowing the people they have selected can do the job. Confidence in judgment is vital for a Significant Manager.

This is different from *overconfidence*. Significant Managers have the humility and perspective to know that the title "manager" does not mean they have all the answers. Although confident in their abilities, they are aware of their challenges and open to advice, new learning, and growth. When managers demonstrate confidence in their own abilities and the abilities of their employees, they encourage the employees to step up, make decisions, and take on more responsibility. In turn, the employees respond and perform.

Here's a great example: There was an organization that ran a team of drivers who operated a linen pickup and delivery service. The Customer Service Manager was asked to take over this team of drivers, many of whom had been with the company for fifteen years or longer. Although the manager knew nothing about delivery trucks, delivery routes, or the type of work that these employees performed, he had the confidence to believe that with hard work and by building relationships with the employees, he could learn the jobs of the drivers and together they could run an efficient and effective department.

What he discovered was that although they were experienced and overall a good team, these drivers were sullen and unhappy. Their department had been overseen in the past by managers who did not respect or care about them. The drivers did just enough not to get fired and didn't really care about the welfare of the company. One of the first challenges the new manager faced was to add a new route to take care of an additional customer, a new hotel. The caveat: He could not hire another driver, pay overtime, or buy another truck. Somehow, he had to make it work with existing resources.

For two weeks, the manager struggled with the route schedule but he could not design one that would allow him to add a delivery within the existing structure. In desperation, he held a staff meeting with his front-line drivers. He explained the challenge, including the restrictions, and asked for ideas. The drivers' response was to sit with their arms crossed, looking at the table. After several minutes of awkward silence, the manager sighed and said, "Well, if any of you has an idea on how we can make this work, I really need your help. Come to my office any time if you think of something."

Toward the end of the day, one of the more experienced drivers came to the manager's office and stood in the doorway, looking like he would turn and run at the slightest provocation. The manager looked up, smiled, and said, "Larry. What can I do for you?" Quietly, Larry said, "I can fix your route problem." The manager was ecstatic. Larry told him how they used to run a particularly difficult route in "the old days" using a "tugger" (a kind of trailer) instead of a truck to get into tight spaces. He suggested that if they went back to that process, he could probably save at least a couple of hours on his route, which would give enough time to add the new route. Larry surprised the manager by saying he would be willing to test the idea for a week and track the timing.

The manager said, "Just tell me what you need and I'll get it for you." The test ran for five days, and Larry's process saved more than four hours on the route using the tugger, more than enough time to add the new delivery and enhance the efficiency of the route as well. Larry was recognized and rewarded for taking the initiative to solve the challenge. And by demonstrating his confidence in Larry, the new manager encouraged the other drivers to step up and share their own ideas.

Significance Exercise #16: Your Managerial Face

What kind of face do you show your people? Ask three people who know you well to rate you for each of the Seven C's of Significant Management. Make the selections and results anonymous so you can get honest opinions. Remember, you're also going to rate yourself as well, then compare your score with the average of the other three.

Ask three subordinates who have worked with you for years to rate you on the Seven C's using a scale of one to ten. Rate yourself in the appropriate box as well. Use the descriptions of each of the Seven C's below.

Compassion The ability to act selflessly to aid another	Clarity Precise, unambiguous understanding of a situation	Composure The ability to look, seem and be calm under all circumstances
Your self-rating: First person's rating: Second person's rating: Third person's rating: Average of the three: _____	Your self-rating: First person's rating: Second person's rating: Third person's rating: Average of the three: _____	Your self-rating: First person's rating: Second person's rating: Third person's rating: Average of the three: _____
Conviction Acting according to principles from which you never deviate	**Character** Being defined by inner qualities such as honesty, strength and commitment	**Confidence** Self-assurance in your own abilities
Your self-rating: First person's rating: Second person's rating: Third person's rating: Average of the three: _____	Your self-rating: First person's rating: Second person's rating: Third person's rating: Average of the three: _____	Your self-rating: First person's rating: Second person's rating: Third person's rating: Average of the three: _____

Courage The fortitude to stay the right course in the face of pressure	Scoring (your average for each C)
Your self-rating: First person's rating: Second person's rating: Third person's rating: Average of the three: _____	8-10: This is one of the strongest areas of your management skill. 5-7: Moderate, but you could improve and bolster your odds of promotion. 1-4: This C is hurting you as a leader. **How did you rate yourself versus the other three? Did you score higher or lower in each area? What does that mean for your self-assessment of your managerial ability?**

7. Courage

A Significant Manager demonstrates courage by adhering to the core values of his or her character during times of stress or uncertainty. It is much easier to demonstrate significance when things are going well, but it is another thing altogether to defy the status quo or swim against conventional wisdom when pressure is coming down from the top or people express doubt about your ideas. Character is demonstrating significance when it is *easy*; courage is demonstrating significance when it is *difficult*.

The courageous manager makes the right, just, or ethical decision even when fear is present. It doesn't matter whether it's fear of repercussions, fear of missed opportunities, or fear of job loss that is the factor. We have seen many examples of decisions within the ranks of large corporations that were self-serving, intended to protect the managers and executives of these corporations.

Not so long ago, this country had what was called the "Big Seven" accounting firms. Today only two of these major accounting firms are in business. The events that led to the demise of five of the most powerful accounting firms in the country were, in some respects and at some levels, brought about by *lack of courage* that can be laid at the doorstep of accounting managers for these firms. Certainly the executives of the firms drove the unethical and illegal business practices that resulted in the downfall of the organizations they led. But as the stories unfolded, it was also clear there were managers at various levels who lacked the courage to do the right thing: to speak up against their leaders when asked to manipulate the books. The same thing happens in politics, education, and science. It is difficult to defy the group.

The accounting managers at these firms lacked courage. They were focused on success rather than significance. Fear of demotion, job loss, or falling from favor with powerful leaders drove them to follow orders despite the fact that they knew the things they were being asked to do were wrong. The end result was, in many cases, greater than any fear they had imagined—prosecution and imprisonment.

Significant Managers have the courage to speak up against their leaders and peers if necessary, to stand by their convictions and not let anyone or any situation sway them from loyalty to their values and beliefs. It is not always easy to have courage and do the right thing when it means speaking up against leaders, peers, and partners in a corporate culture where abject loyalty is expected and acceptance is of prime importance.

Next Steps for Significance Seekers...

- *... What did you think of your last manager? How do you compare to him or her?*

- *... Do you show the same face to your subordinates and your superiors, or do you act differently around each group?*

- *... Write down your convictions as they apply to the company and give a copy to each person under your supervision.*

- *... Write up your best ideas for how the organization could improve and share them with your superiors.*

- *... Encourage the people below you to do the same with you.*

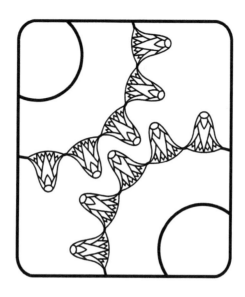

CHAPTER TEN
The Seven Strengths of a Significant Employee

KEY FACETS OF PERSONAL SIGNIFICANCE FROM THE PERSPECTIVE OF THE FRONT-LINE EMPLOYEE, AND WAYS ANYONE CAN BECOME SIGNIFICANT

> *The biggest job we have is to teach a newly hired employee how to fail intelligently. We have to train him to experiment over and over and to keep on trying and failing until he learns what will work.*
> —*Charles F. Kettering, American engineer*

For front-line employees, significance is a surprisingly simple thing. However, it is not easy. If you remember significance is about pursuits that expand your vision and enhance the world around you, achieving it requires employees to find and practice the balance between commitment to their personal goals and commitment to the organization. When seeking significance, front-line employees will choose companies whose values align with their personal values.

A Significant Employee exhibits the same attributes as the Significant Manager or Leader, but from an individual perspective. Whereas the Significant Manager finds significance through his or her interactions with employees, colleagues, and superiors, the front-line employee finds significance through his or her personal values and beliefs, which drive individual actions, attitudes, and ultimately performance in professional and personal life. Put simply, the Significant Employee has found a way to serve cherished personal goals and passions via the professional environment.

A stack of management and leadership books tall enough to block out the sun tells us that great leadership creates dedicated and loyal employees who are driven to succeed for the good of the organization. I disagree. Great leaders do not *create* great employees. Instead, great leadership brings out the *significance* in employees who are innately driven to find their own significance. If an employee is not oriented toward significance, it is possible for gifted, highly aware managers and leaders to evoke the potential for significance in that person, but it does not always work. To paraphrase therapists and life coaches, you have to *want* to change. Even the most skilled Significant Leader cannot bring out the desire for significance in an employee who is blindly focused on nothing but shallow success. There are those who choose to be average.

But those who choose significance are the role models for Significant Employees. Their personal values and beliefs dictate their actions, and their actions exemplify the essence of their being and how they see themselves fitting into the organization, the community, and society at large. Significant Employees take direction from their hearts, not from managers and leaders. Premier organizations that are known for their positive cultures and exceptional customer service do everything within their power to lure these people to their organizations, realizing you can train just about anyone to perform a task, but you cannot train significance. You can bring it out and stoke its fires, but if it's not there at all, no magic words will make it appear.

Leaders and managers of successful organizations know their role is to provide support and guidance for the Significant Employee and trust that person to make good decisions and do the right things … even if that means leaving the organization. It's important to understand that even the most Significant Employees cannot demonstrate their significance if they do not have an environment that provides the freedom to act according to their values. Significant Employees will seek out organizations that give them the freedom to act in a way that demonstrates their values.

Significance Exercise #17: You're the CEO

If you were the head of an organization instead of an employee, how would you apply the values, beliefs, and convictions that make you significant? Here's your chance.

Write down up to four of your core principles, values, or guiding beliefs. Then describe how you would apply them to change your company's direction, culture, or very nature.

Core Value #1:

How I would apply it to the organization:

Core Value #2:

How I would apply it to the organization:

Core Value #3:

How I would apply it to the organization:

Core Value #4:

How I would apply it to the organization:

> *We need to find ways to capture the creative and innovative spirit of the American worker. That's the real organizational challenge.*
>
> —Paul Allaire, former CEO of Xerox
>
> *Everything we do must start out with a recognition of a balance between work and family. The only sustainable competitive advantage a company has is its employees.*
>
> —Jerre Stead, CEO of National Cash Register

Lucky Seven

The Seven Strengths are the same for the Significant Employee as for leaders and managers. The difference lies in how they are expressed.

1. Compassion

What does it look like when a front-line employee demonstrates compassion? The following stories illustrate how employees, through their actions, behaviors, and compassionate, caring attitudes, find their significance through compassion.

> *Maggie, a phlebotomist at Florida's Blood Centers, shows empathy for donors who are afraid of giving blood but want to present this special gift to the community. One donor in particular needs extra time and attention. She will give blood but cannot stand the sight of the blood or the feel of the tube that is transferring the blood on her skin. This donor always asks for Maggie when she comes to donate. When asked about her experience, this donor says Maggie makes her feel special. Maggie remembers her name and does not ridicule her for her fear. She takes extra time with her, makes cheerful conversation, tells her when to avoid looking, and puts a towel under the tube and another one over the tube so the donor does not feel it or see it. The last time this donor came to give blood, Maggie was on her way to a much-deserved break on a very busy day. When she recognized the donor, she postponed her break so she could personally take care of her....*
>
> *A woman entered a casino in California. It was her first time visiting this casino, so she wanted to acquire a player's club card to accrue points for special offers. When she approached the counter to sign up for the card, she was greeted with a big smile and a friendly "Hello." The casino employee gave the woman an*

application to register for her card, and it was at this point the woman realized she had left her glasses in the hotel room. She could not see the application well enough to fill out the information, so she handed it back to the employee and told her she would apply at another time, explaining about the reading glasses. The employee said, "No problem! I bought an extra pair of reading glasses and I keep it here just for customers. ..."

A housekeeper at Walt Disney World's Polynesian Resort heard that a guest was sick with the flu and had to stay in the room while her family visited the theme parks. The housekeeper went to the kitchen, got a bowl of soup, and took it to the guest with a get well card. ...

Another time, a guest at a Disney hotel (working in Orlando, I hear a lot of Disney stories) came to Walt Disney World with her family. It was her first vacation since back surgery. She was feeling well when she arrived, but the extra activity reinjured her back. She was stuck in the hotel room for five days. A housekeeper heard about the room-bound guest and brought magazines and books from home for her to read. She also made time in her schedule to visit with the guest and keep her company. ...

A food server at a restaurant was involved in a terrible car accident. She was in intensive care for some time and in the hospital for three weeks. While she was incapacitated, her fellow employees took turns shuttling her small children to and from the day care and ran errands for her and her family. ...

These stories show it is the small gestures from the heart that create significance. Like Significant Leaders and Managers, Significant Employees exemplify compassion and show empathy toward customers and fellow employees. Compassion means following the Golden Rule and treating others as you would like to be treated. Wise organizations and managers reward and encourage such behavior.

2. Clarity

With clear vision you may see where you are going, but without strong, articulated values, it may not be worth making the trip.

  —Bill Capodagli and Lynn Jackson, speakers and experts on Disney culture

Effort and courage are not enough without direction and purpose.

  —John F. Kennedy, thirty-fifth U.S. president

For the front-line employee, clarity is about aligning personal values with the organization's values. Employees who have clarity understand the organization's vision and mission and understand how they, through their actions and values, contribute to achieving key goals. They clearly understand their role and know who they serve, how they contribute and what is expected of them. They not only sincerely want to contribute in a meaningful way to the success of the company, they *enjoy* doing it.

I was once on a Southwest Airlines flight heading home from California. The plane had several children on their way to Orlando excited about visiting the theme parks. After the obligatory safety announcements, I observed the flight attendants interacting with the children and talking to them about their plans for vacation. Suddenly, a flight attendant announced on the PA system: "Boys and girls, I am about to perform my very famous magic trick, never before seen since the last flight! Kids, you'll need to have a good view of the aisle. You may get up on your knees if necessary. First, I must go into my secret magic room to prepare."

With that, he ducked into the lavatory at the front of the plane and emerged holding the end of the roll of tissue in his hand. He walked down the aisle, trailing the tissue along behind him, singing and waving at the kids who were laughing at this grown man's silly behavior. About two-thirds of the way down the aisle, he laid the tissue on the floor, encouraging the kids in the back of the plane to move to the aisle so they could see. He then straddled the tissue and did a funny run back to the "magic room." He leaned out of the lavatory and said over the speaker, "Watch carefully now as I make this trail of tissue disappear." With that, he flushed the toilet and the tissue zipped up the aisle into the lavatory and vanished. As you can imagine, the kids went crazy. The applause and cheers from everyone on the plane prompted him to take several bows.

This story is a perfect example of an employee who has found significance, understanding that his job was more than attending to the physical comfort of the passengers. He made people laugh, made a long flight less tedious, and it was obvious that he gained as much enjoyment as the passengers from his actions. More importantly, Southwest Airlines has given him "permission" to demonstrate his significance with customers. Smart company.

Clarity means employees know not only their core values but the core values of the company. That means the company makes its core values clear and communicates them to each person through its actions. When this happens, employees take pride in providing meaningful services and products to customers. They thrive on their relationships with fellow workers, partners, and customers and are strong team players. Their work has a purpose they respect and believe in, and as a result they do better work, enjoy it more, have better morale, and stay with the company longer.

On the other hand, if the Significant Employee does not feel that his or her purpose aligns with the company's, that person will become unhappy and disillusioned, often choosing to leave the company. This is the challenge of working with people who are on the significance path. They are continually seeking an alignment of their values and organizational values. Organizations that nurture and respect this alignment have the most success in retaining Significant Employees and ultimately experience the most success in business.

Significance Story

Walt Disney World receives tens of thousands of guest letters each year. The majority of the letters are compliments, and the majority of the compliments are very specific to some action an employee took to create a "Magical Experience." Here is one of those stories as shared by my friend who worked at Walt Disney World for more than thirty-four years:

"I loved to interact with the guests who came to visit the Magic Kingdom. I would always ask them about their experience and, as a result, often heard wonderful stories of magical experiences delivered by front-line Cast Members. On one occasion, I met a man and woman who had a small boy, four years old. As I usually do, I asked about their visit and said I hoped they were having a good time. The woman told me their trip to Disney was more wonderful than they'd ever expected. She was eager to share this story with me.

"She said, 'Early this morning, we arrived in the Magic Kingdom with reservations for the princess breakfast in the top of the castle. My son, Mikey, has a huge crush on Princess Jasmine. As we were having our breakfast, the princesses came out to greet everyone. Mikey spotted Jasmine immediately. Apparently, our server told Jasmine about Mikey's crush and she made a beeline to our table.

'At first, Mikey was really shy, but after a few minutes Jasmine persuaded him to give her a big hug and she planted a little kiss on his cheek. Mikey was beside himself with excitement. Later that day, we were sitting on the curb for the parade and as the floats came by, Mikey was waving frantically at Jasmine as she approached in her snow globe. She turned at just the right

moment, noticed Mikey on the curb, and gave him a big wave and a smile, saying, "Hi, Mikey!" She then blew him a kiss. He was so excited that she remembered him! We will always remember our trip to Walt Disney World.'

"As this woman was telling me her story, she had tears in her eyes and so did I. As it turns out, the man and woman had never told Jasmine Mikey's name. He had a name tag with emergency contact information pinned to his shirt in the event that he became separated from his parents. Jasmine had taken note of the tag and remembered his name."

3. Composure

For a front-line employee, maintaining composure is often as simple as staying calm while interacting with an irate customer or peer. This is rarely easy. Many companies train people vigorously to deal with these occurrences. There is no doubt that this type of training is valuable and employees benefit from the guidance they receive. But what if an organization were to provide *no* training for dealing with an irate customer or peer?

You would see the Significant Employee stand out from all others. Significant Employees seem to know how to handle these situations. They have an innate calm and poise that is driven by their value system. They stay cool, listen, do not take the situation personally, and make good decisions to solve the issue for the customer or peer. I would suggest this is because they are fundamentally happy with what they are doing and so have no need to lash out at a customer to express their anger or frustration.

If you ask them why they handled the situation as they did, they would say things like, "He was just upset. It wasn't his fault. He just wanted someone to listen." The Significant Employee with composure lives by the phrase, "The customer may not always be right but must be allowed to be wrong with dignity."

As with leaders and managers, composure for a front-line employee also means staying calm during stressful situations and in a crisis. Just as managers, they may be required to make good decisions when a lot is on the line. The Significant Employee will not only put into play the policies, processes, and training that person has learned, but will also implement the decisions from higher up and have a great deal to do with whether those decisions fail or succeed.

> *The beauty of the soul shines out when a man bears with composure one heavy mischance after another, not because he does not feel them, but because he is a man of high and heroic temper.*
>
> —*Aristotle, Greek philosopher*

4. Conviction

Think about the passengers of Flight 93 on September 11th. During this horrifying flight, these passengers, following their convictions, chose to take action, knowing this would likely result in the ultimate sacrifice. Many called their loved ones to explain the situation and say goodbye. Under unimaginable circumstances, they implemented a plan that saved many other people and probably prevented a catastrophic plane crash into the U.S. Capitol.

Challenging inefficient processes, policies, and the status quo, and thinking innovatively, are natural for employees who are living in significance. They do what they know is right, despite the risks. They have their convictions, driven by their personal values, and do not waver from those beliefs. If Significant Employees are working for an organization that does not have a positive culture driven by a strong value system, they risk threats, discipline, or even termination for deviating from policy—and will likely do things their way regardless. Their need to adhere to their moral code is stronger than their need to preserve one short-term job.

This story illustrates that mindset. A young woman I know got married and moved with her husband to Missouri, where he had an excellent job offer. The young couple were saving for a house of their own, so after arriving in their small town of Pevely, the woman began job hunting. However, there were very few jobs available. After interviewing for a position at the local bank, she was happy to be hired and thought this would be the perfect job. Her hours and pay were good and she would have a lot of customer interaction, which she liked very much. It was not long before she had built relationships with several customers and often had a line of regulars who wanted only her to take care of their banking transactions.

During her training, she was told one of her responsibilities was to "upsell" bank customers, persuading them to invest money in various funds, money markets, etc., with the bank. Not thinking much about it and with a strong work ethic, she vowed to be a good employee. She was given goals for achieving monthly quotas and told her job performance would be rated on her ability to meet or exceed these quotas. She soon discovered she was expected to meet these sales quotas even if it meant selling products that were not good investments for customers in order to meet the bank's sales objectives.

On one occasion, she was taking care of one of her regular customers, an elderly man she knew lived on a fixed income. He often said she reminded him of his granddaughter and she had also become very fond of him. This month, there were certain bonds all tellers were supposed to sell to the customers. However, on this occasion, the young woman made no attempt to sell the bond to the elderly gentleman. When the customer left the counter, her manager, who had been observing her from the back of the room, approached her and berated her for not doing her job. He was quick to point out that she was behind in her sales quotas and that her job was in jeopardy.

After accusing her of being lazy, the manager demanded an explanation. Her answer was that she knew this gentleman did not have the money to invest. She also stated that the customer trusted her and if she had recommended the bond, he may have diverted finances he could not afford to the bond. She did not want to have this on her conscience and told the manager she refused to push sales if it was the wrong thing to do.

She was promptly fired. While at first being fired was devastating, she realized she would not have stayed long in a job that insisted on her committing actions that went against her beliefs and values. Ironically, she was exactly the kind of employee that would have boosted the bank's fortunes.

Employees with strong convictions who find that their leaders do not share them eventually leave. The young woman in the story above ultimately would have decided of her own volition to leave the bank. The values of the organization required that employees sacrifice significance for success. Significant Employees find it untenable to remain with an organization whose policies do not align with their values and, except under extreme circumstances, living their values transcends even the need for a paycheck.

Employees may reject a promotion to a management position because they value life balance with their family and understand that in order to succeed as a manager, they would be required to make sacrifices, such as less time with family, more stress, or less time for spiritual or charitable activities.

> *If it is once again one against forty-eight, then I am very sorry for the forty-eight.*
> —*Margaret Thatcher, former British Prime Minister*

5. Character

What you are thunders so loudly that I cannot hear what you say.
　　　　　—Ralph Waldo Emerson, nineteenth century American poet

Everyone tries to define this thing called Character. It's not hard. Character is doing what's right when nobody's looking.
　　　　　—J.C. Watts Jr., contemporary American writer

You don't get character because you're successful; you build character because of the hardships you face.
　　　　　—Herman Edwards, head coach of the New York Jets

Truth is knowing that your character is shaped by everyday choices.
　　　　　—Vince Lombardi, NFL head coach

As we stated in the chapter on Significant Managers, conviction is *establishing* what is important to you; character is *living it*. The same is true when describing Significant Employees. Ask yourself this question: Based on my choices and actions, would my fellow employees be able to identify my values? Significant Employees have the kind of character that is evident every day in the things they say and the actions they take.

Your true self becomes clear to all through your actions. In the award-winning television show *Ugly Betty*, the main character has the conviction to be true to herself, and as a significant person, true to her character. She is consistent in the expression of her values; they don't change depending on the situation. Her character is exemplified by the choices she makes for herself and others, despite the fact that they often draw derision from her fellow workers. This show, which is all about character that isn't visible from the outside, has been applauded for setting a good example for young girls. In our society, young girls especially are judged by their physical appearance and by whether or not their behaviors fit into the "norm" established by society. The example set by Betty in this show exemplifies what it means to be a Significant Employee of real character.

By the way, Significant Employees don't take sole credit for their team's success. They are more interested in sharing the spotlight with their team members. They take responsibility when they slip up, and not only admit mistakes and learn from their mistakes, but share what they have learned with their peers and superiors. Employees of significant character take personal responsibility for their actions and hold themselves and others accountable to high standards. They are often the moral and ethical compasses for the people around them.

They treat everyone with respect regardless of religion, sexual orientation, age, or race. They refuse to listen to and engage in office gossip. This Significant Employee is the cashier at the mall who invited three co-workers to her family's home for Thanksgiving because she didn't want them to be alone on the holiday. It is the teenage boy who defended another teenager with mental disabilities against the bully on the bus.

The Architects

As part of a career week at school, a middle-school boy was out job-shadowing at a local architecture firm. He'd always loved to draw and was amazed by the big buildings in the city, but today he hoped to see what exactly it was that architects do. He walked up to the first architect he saw and asked, "What are you doing?" The man said, "I'm just drawing." The boy kept walking and came across another architect working on a computer. "What are you working on?" the boy asked. "I'm developing a 3-D model of a classroom," the man replied. A bit closer to discovering what it was the architects were working on, the boy continued walking and came across a third man. "What are you doing?" the boy asked again. The third architect turned to him, smiling. He seemed to be the happiest of the three, and said, "I'm helping build a school so kids like you can learn what they want to be when they grow up."

---

6. Confidence

> *Believe in yourself. Have faith in your abilities! Without a humble but reasonable confidence in your own powers, you cannot be successful or happy.*
>
> —*Norman Vincent Peale, author and Protestant preacher*

You cannot mandate confidence; it comes from within. Employees who demonstrate significance through confidence are highly sought-after. They are often referred to as "self-starters" because they don't need the reassurance of a superior's OK to make things happen. They are the innovators, the groundbreakers, and the ones who shake up a company and stand out in tough times. Employees with a lot of confidence have character and convictions that are driven by their values. This is the compass that guides them, giving them the confidence to make decisions and act on their beliefs for the good of others and the organization. When they are doing what they feel is right, they will not shy away from risk or duck confrontation.

Don't get me wrong. It is true great managers and leaders can develop confidence in front-line employees by providing the support and mentorship that enable them to feel safe in their work environment. We have talked about the positive impact Significant Leaders have on their organizations in this regard. But you cannot instill the fundamentally deep network of values that underlie confidence; those come from experience, upbringing, and a conscious decision to live by one's choices, come what may.

However, poor leaders can erode or even destroy employee confidence through repeated criticisms, micromanagement, demonstrations of lack of trust, and outright abusive behavior. So what is the difference between the employee who has confidence that is nurtured by great leadership and the confidence exhibited by a Significant Employee? The Significant Employee's confidence borders on messianic zeal and is practically impossible to destroy because it comes from within. It is driven by his or her essence of being. In fact, it *is* his or her essence of being.

This is what Abraham Maslow called a *self-actualizing* person. Individuals like this are no longer driven by a need to prove themselves, either to themselves or to anyone else. Self-actualizers have powerful self-esteem that allows them to create their own meaning and purpose in their lives. Their work, their activities, and their very existence have value, because they know they are making a significant contribution to themselves and to others.

Organizations with a culture that fosters courageous leadership and an environment of trust have the best chance of attracting and retaining the front-line employee who demonstrates significance through confidence. These employees add tremendous value to the organization and can be directly responsible for successful business results.

Significance Exercise #18: Your Strengths

What are your strengths? Do you see yourself the same way others do? Complete this exercise (which is oddly similar to the ones in the Leader and Manager chapters) and you'll find out.

Ask three colleagues who have worked with you for years to rate you on the Seven C's using a scale of one to ten. Rate yourself in the appropriate box as well. Consider keeping names off the ratings to avoid hard feelings. Use the descriptions of each of the Seven C's below.

Compassion The ability to act selflessly to aid another	Clarity Precise, unambiguous understanding of a situation	Composure The ability to look, seem and be calm under all circumstances
Your self-rating: First person's rating: Second person's rating: Third person's rating: Average of the three: _____	Your self-rating: First person's rating: Second person's rating: Third person's rating: Average of the three: _____	Your self-rating: First person's rating: Second person's rating: Third person's rating: Average of the three: _____
Conviction Acting according to principles from which you never deviate	**Character** Being defined by inner qualities such as honesty, strength, and commitment	**Confidence** Self-assurance in your own abilities
Your self-rating: First person's rating: Second person's rating: Third person's rating: Average of the three: _____	Your self-rating: First person's rating: Second person's rating: Third person's rating: Average of the three: _____	Your self-rating: First person's rating: Second person's rating: Third person's rating: Average of the three: _____
Courage The fortitude to stay the right course in the face of pressure	**Scoring (your average for each C)**	
Your self-rating: First person's rating: Second person's rating: Third person's rating: Average of the three: _____	8-10: This is an area that makes you a real asset. 5-7: You have room to improve here, and a great deal of potential. 1-4: This is an area that's holding you back from becoming a manager. **How did you rate yourself versus the other three? Did you score higher or lower in each area? What does that mean for your self-assessment of your abilities as an employee?**	

7. Courage

All progress has resulted from people who took unpopular positions.
　　　　　—Adlai E. Stevenson, twentieth century Democratic politician

One man with courage makes a majority.
　　　　　—Andrew Jackson, seventh U.S. president

Courage is contagious. When a brave man takes a stand, the spines of others are stiffened.
　　　　　—Rev. Billy Graham, Southern Baptist preacher and evangelist

It takes real fortitude and strength for an employee to show courage—that is, stand by his or her core values and character even in the face of pressure, crisis, or conflict. For a leader or manager, position can shield him or her from some consequences; there is always a buck to pass. But if you're a cubicle dweller on the front lines with customers, you take the heat personally. Sticking to your guns can be harrowing. Significant Employees are willing to fight the good fight.

Employees often shine with significance when they persevere in excellence despite personal issues that may be taking precedence over their focus on work and work goals. A Significant Employee has the courage to speak up when he or she believes something is wrong. A perfect example is the whistle-blowers who have faced ostracizing from peers and retaliation from employers, yet who demonstrate tremendous courage in holding to their convictions and speaking out in the pursuit of justice. They do not know the meaning of the words, "It's not my job, it's not my problem, I'm going to keep my head down and hope no one notices me!" They stand up boldly to protect others and to preserve ethical business practices, even in the face of adversity or possible repercussions to themselves.

We can all learn a lesson from a story by Robert Levering, a San Francisco-based writer who co-authored the book *The 100 Best Companies to Work for in America*:

> *Not long ago, I came across a book that helped me appreciate what makes good workplaces tick. In* The Gift, *poet and essayist Lewis Hyde provides an explanation for the place of creativity in our market-oriented society. Hyde puts forth the idea that a work of art is a gift rather than a commodity. Works of art, therefore, exist in two parallel economies—the market economy and the gift economy. The market economy is governed by the law of supply and demand. A painting, for example,*

may be sold for a thousand dollars at an auction. But the painting also has a separate life as a gift. Aside from the subjective aspect of the artist's gift (or talent) needed to create the work, those who view the work consider it a gift: "Even if we have paid a fee at the door of a museum or concert hall, when we are touched by a work of art something comes to us which has nothing to do with the price ... the work appeals, as Joseph Conrad says, to a part of our being which is itself a gift and not an acquisition."

Hyde goes on: "It is the cardinal difference between gift and commodity exchange that a gift establishes a feeling-bond between two people, while the sale of a commodity leaves no necessary connection. Both sides recognize that whenever a gift is given, the giver is giving part of himself, which helps to explain the basis for the feeling-bond between parties of a gift exchange."

When reading this, I was struck by the similarities between what happens in great workplaces and his description of the operation of a gift economy. Interactions between company and employees are acted out according to implicit rules that both sides understand as being somewhat like the unstated rules of gift exchanges.

The analogy of the gift economy strikes a resonant chord for another important reason: Human work is not just a commodity. Work encompasses individual initiative and creativity. When people work, as opposed to merely laboring for money, they are offering part of what they consider their individual essence, part of what distinguishes them as human beings. Work cannot be so carefully circumscribed as a simple time-for-money exchange.

Note, however, that it is precisely the gift-like nature of work that allows an insensitive employer to completely ignore the human element of his relationship with the workers: A gift can be refused. What makes good workplaces special is that the company recognizes the possibilities of gift-like exchanges with employees and actively cultivates those interactions.

If you would like to run an organization full of average employees, run your company as a commodity-driven exchange. However, if you understand that to survive in business today you must attract and retain significant employees, you may want to consider running your company from the perspective of a gift exchange, creating bonds with and appreciation for your employees.

Next Steps for Significance Seekers...

- *... Next time you are in a meeting or at an employee gathering, ask everyone who has integrity to raise his or her hand. You will notice that all people raise their hands. Ask them to put their hands down and raise their hands if they believe everyone with whom they work has integrity. You may see a few hands raised, but not all. This activity represents our personal view of self. But why the disparity between how we view ourselves and how we view others? The answer is that we rate ourselves based on our intentions; others rate us based on our behaviors.*

CHAPTER ELEVEN
Go Forth With Hope

HOW TO CREATE A LEGACY THAT ENDURES WHEN WE ARE GONE AND RECOGNIZE THE TEACHABLE MOMENTS THAT ARISE WHEN WE ARE FOCUSED ON SIGNIFICANCE

No legacy is so rich as honesty.
—William Shakespeare, British poet and playwright

A legacy is the residue of a life well-lived. It can be a monetary inheritance to family members, a philanthropic gift to charity, or a company or research that others may build upon after the individual's demise. But a significant legacy adds another residual benefit: people who have been inspired by your example. A significant life lives on through many generations that follow it through the personal impact it has made upon the lives of others. Each day you live a significant life is a teaching moment you can use to educate by example and show others how marvelous, rich, and joyous life can be.

Death is not a subject most Americans like to talk about. We don't like to think about the end of life when we are in the hustle and bustle of it. However, people of significance have learned that life is a lot like gardening. There are times we plant, times we prune and times we harvest. The most precious crops will be from those tiny seeds we planted along the way that are harvested long after our lives are over. A significant life plants seeds in the lives of people, which will later produce the legacy of a rich, plentiful harvest of good, which in turn reaches out to change the lives of even more people. Think about diverse individuals from Abraham Lincoln to Rosa Parks and you'll get an idea of what I mean.

> **Legacy:** *A structure, organization, or model of behavior that inspires and motivates others to continue your work after your death.*

Throughout history, there have been examples of extraordinary people who, through their good deeds and admirable actions, have left such an impression that their memories have lasted through generations and transcended gender, age, and race. These historical icons—such titans as Thomas Jefferson, Eleanor Roosevelt, and Susan B. Anthony—left a legacy of hope due to their courage and compassion for all people. They were true embodiments of the qualities we talked about in the previous chapters. Or, it might be more accurate to say these qualities are based on the characteristics of selfless people and leaders like them.

Bear in mind, however, that you do not have to be a world-famous freedom fighter, a famed humanitarian, or a pious peacekeeper in order to leave your legacy. There is only one Nelson Mandela, one Jonas Salk. You only have to have the desire to leave an inspiring legacy and the drive to do good. Good deeds, like people, come in all shapes and sizes. And just like people, no one deed is better than the other, as long as the intent behind it is a genuine one. Remember, the smallest seed can grow into the biggest tree. Similarly, the smallest action or sign of compassion can give rise to the greatest hope. All you need is the desire to serve others, even if it is in the smallest of ways.

If you were to examine the lives of most Significant Leaders, you'd find that their personal missions often tied into a simple belief that led them to a life of service.

Martin Luther King Jr.—Equality for all people
Mother Teresa—Charity to the poorest and weakest
Mohandas Gandhi—Social justice and independence for the oppressed
Marie Curie—Education
Aleksandr Solzhenitsyn—Freedom of speech
Nelson Mandela—Equality for all people

These are not complex ideas. What allowed these people to leave world-changing legacies through simple convictions? *Awareness and commitment.* That may sound simplistic, but in our society, where thousands of messages compete for our attention and our own egos and needs often take precedence, it is easy to ignore the important things going on around us. Awareness occurs when we are mindful of injustices occurring around us, privy to the pain that others endure, and sensitive to the needs of others. Once you are aware, you can commit to action, using your passions and talents to determine how you can fill a need.

Significance Exercise #19: What is Your Legacy?

We may not always think about our legacy, but we all want to know that as we live, we are leaving a meaningful trail behind us to inspire others. As Dr. Martin Luther King Jr. and other great people have done, what kind of legacy do you think you are leaving today?

First, describe the legacy you have built so far based on your actions and decisions to date. Next, describe the kind of significant legacy you would like to create going forward and how you might make it happen.

My legacy to date: (example: a monetary inheritance)

The legacy I would like to leave:
(example: a mission and foundation for aiding children in poverty)

How I could make that happen starting now:

Take for instance, the blood donor in our opening story. He was aware of the dire need for blood donors, and his drive to give someone a second chance at life impelled him to make blood donation a habit. There may be millions of donors out there like him. His name is not known by those whose lives he saves. He won't be in the history books. But by striving to surpass superficial success by constantly considering the lives of others, he has made the ultimate difference in the lives of who knows how many people. Many lives will be touched because he chose to pursue a passion and make others a part of his life journey.

> **Mission:** *The specific goal that springs out of your life's purpose, the thing you were put on this earth to achieve.*

Your Legacy

How will you leave your legacy? What are your passions and principles, and who are you helping through them? Who are you sharing them with so they can carry on your work after you are gone?

As we pursue a life of significance and focus on creating a legacy through the lives of others, it is important for us to realize that life is not a constant flow of positive energy and favorable events. While pursuing significance provides clarity of purpose and equips you with the qualities needed to realize a higher calling, it is essential to remember that life is not always easy.

The ocean demonstrates for us the flow or "tides" of life. It demonstrates that even as we align our energies and our intent, there will be both times of great abundance and times of great adversity. Just as there are low tide and high tide, stormy seas and calm waters, the rhythms of life command our respect. People seeking significance know they should not try to control the natural world. If the tide ebbs or we find ourselves in a moment of emptiness or hardship, we must honor it with the same fortitude with which we embrace opportunity or good fortune. In moments when there is a stillness to the sea, we should welcome the chance for quiet, solitude, self-reflection, clarity, and the discoveries that can be unearthed during the ebb after the high tide recedes.

Nothing is permanent except for the fact that the ocean exists. The same is true for us. Life always exists; we will not. In our lives (religious considerations aside) nothing lasts forever except for the actions that spring from our values and character. If we sail the seas of life in a vessel of significance, we are able to remain strong and whole, thriving in spite of the conditions that surround us. In addition, we can correlate our lives to the waves that we cannot control. Sometimes the waves and wind will be gentle and we will ride high; other times violent storms will toss and terrify us and bring us to the brink of abandoning everything. But if we have the proper perspective and the desire for significance, we can see the truth:

Even the storm-tossed waves are always taking us somewhere.

We are always on a journey, and if we face it with honor and strength, even the rough times can change us in ways that reveal great beauty and courage, making us better leaders, managers, employees, and people.

With all of this said, there are books on self-improvement that try to address and provide set formulas for "success." While there is some value in using these road maps in certain areas of our lives, the lessons in this book stand out because it is critical that each of us seek and find our own interpretations of "significance." Regardless of your age, profession, religion, or station in life, significance is a universal calling in each of us, played out differently by each individual. Significance fills the void within by providing a framework for meaning, purpose, joy, and the creation of that which is greater than we.

It's time for you to chart your own course through life's ocean. What will you take with you as you venture out? Where will you go? I hope you will begin to understand it is not the grandeur or visibility of the things you do that makes them significant, but the degree to which they make the world sweeter, safer, or more healing for someone else. That may be the ultimate measure of your significance: the number of people who look at you with gratitude and say, "Today is a little better for me than yesterday because of what you did."

Next Steps for Significance Seekers...

- *... List as many as ten actions you could take in the next month that would bring you closer to significance.*

- *... List as many as ten actions you could take in the next quarter that would bring the people around you closer to significance.*

- *... Vow to change one longstanding habit forever.*

- *... Help as many as ten people in ways that do not involve donating money.*

- *... Develop a mantra, a personal statement of self-belief that you can repeat for strength and focus.*

- *...Smile. Dream. Play. Give. Love. See beauty.*

Epilogue

Thank you for taking time to read this book. I hope you will stay in touch, share your stories with me, and allow me to offer some guidance if you reach a point where you're not sure what your next step toward significance should be. I invite you, when you finish this book, to visit www.SimplySignificant.com to view a special video greeting from me. While you're there, please share your own story of your pursuit of significance. It fills me with joy to hear how the ideas in this book have shaped the paths of others.

As you go out into the world, I leave you with this final thought: Remember, your light shines so brightly not for your own sake, but that you should light the way for others. Thank you for bringing light into my world and letting me share mine with you.

Bonus Offer

The author, Anne K. Chinoda, has prepared a personal video message for you to view after reading *Simply Significant*. She also has a special gift for you to download that will help you continue on your own personal journey of significance.

To view this video and download your free gift, visit

www.SimplySignificant.com/bonus

Bring *Simply Significant* to Your Organization

Anne K. Chinoda provides winning strategies for life and leadership in keynotes and presentations based on the *Simply Significant* philosophy and methodology. Anne also offers presentations and interactive training focused on each of the specific aspects of significant leadership. All programs can be customized to meet your organization's unique goals and objectives. For more information, visit www.SimplySignificant.com.

About the Author

Anne K. Chinoda, President and CEO of Florida's Blood Centers (FBC), is a highly sought after public speaker delivering speeches and presentations on nearly every continent around the world. She is frequently engaged to collaborate with international organizations addressing significant health issues and she provides organizations and business leaders with unique leadership training, development, and coaching.

Anne oversees the operations and a multi-million dollar budget for the largest blood center in Florida. She is a proven leader in the field of healthcare with a twenty-three year track record of establishing new benchmarks. Her record is highlighted by outstanding business performance, operational excellence, innovative management, industry leadership, integrated technology, and globalization.

Raised in California, Anne spent her formative years as a competitive figure skater winning numerous championships. After receiving her bachelor's degree from Boston College, Anne found her calling in community service and servant leadership through the inspiration of the Jesuit education and a number of influential philosophers that she studied with in school. As such, she set upon a professional course defined by her passion for human service on an international scale.

Under Anne's leadership, FBC has doubled in size to $125 million, through organic growth and acquisitions. FBC continues to set new standards for the industry in collections, manufacturing, and research, and has engaged innovative systems for enterprise management and lean manufacturing standards.

She has held a number of leadership positions in the blood industry, serving on the boards for America's Blood Centers, the American Association of Blood Banks, and the Florida Association of Blood Banks. Through her industry work, Anne has engaged with international leaders throughout the world for the "globalization" of blood, as they attempt to develop standards and protocols that would allow for blood to move freely throughout the world in the event of a pandemic or other large scale catastrophic event.

Combining her education with a lifetime of work in healthcare and her international work, Anne has become inspired as a "global citizen" to enact change in how people, organizations and other cultures work together across the globe to solve problems and achieve greater results for their efforts. She sees many of these opportunities within her work in the burgeoning life science cluster in Florida.

She has been instrumental in advancing her home state as a hub for life sciences and biotechnology, serving as a board member for BioFlorida and founding board member of bioOrlando. She has developed partnerships with new research institutes in Florida, including the Burnham Institute for Medical Research and Scripps Research Institute. She was appointed by the Florida Speaker of the House to the Scripps Funding Oversight Board. Anne has also worked to develop international relationships for Florida with life science organizations in Germany, Montreal, and Dubai. In 2008, she established key relationships in United Arab Emirates to develop a pioneering new program to expand new research, education and training opportunities in all parts of the Middle East and the United States.

She currently lives in Orlando, Florida, and is married with two sons.

Anne received her Master's of Business degree from Webster University. In Central Florida, Anne serves as chair for the Florida Hospital Cardiovascular Foundation board, which provides philanthropic support for one of the nation's top cardiovascular programs. She has been named Business Executive of the Year by the *Orlando Business Journal,* also receiving that organization's prestigious Women Who Mean Business award. The Rotary Club of Orlando recognized her as Business Woman of the Year; the Public Relations Society of America's Orlando Chapter presented her with a Frank R. Stansberry Ethics Award; and WMFE-TV PBS (Public Broadcasting Services) named her a "Speaking of Women's Health" honoree for significant contributions to community health.

BUY A SHARE OF THE FUTURE IN YOUR COMMUNITY

These certificates make great holiday, graduation and birthday gifts that can be personalized with the recipient's name. The cost of one S.H.A.R.E. or one square foot is $54.17. The personalized certificate is suitable for framing and will state the number of shares purchased and the amount of each share, as well as the recipient's name. The home that you participate in "building" will last for many years and will continue to grow in value.

Here is a sample SHARE certificate:

HABITAT FOR HUMANITY

THIS CERTIFIES THAT

YOUR NAME HERE

HAS INVESTED IN A HOME FOR A DESERVING FAMILY

1985-2005

TWENTY YEARS OF BUILDING FUTURES IN OUR COMMUNITY ONE HOME AT A TIME

1200 SQUARE FOOT HOUSE @ $65,000 = $54.17 PER SQUARE FOOT
This certificate represents a tax deductible donation. It has no cash value.

YES, I WOULD LIKE TO HELP!

I support the work that Habitat for Humanity does and I want to be part of the excitement! As a donor, I will receive periodic updates on your construction activities but, more importantly, I know my gift will help a family in our community realize the dream of homeownership. **I would like to SHARE in your efforts against substandard housing in my community!** *(Please print below)*

PLEASE SEND ME _____ SHARES at $54.17 EACH = $ $_____

In Honor Of: _____

Occasion: (Circle One)   *HOLIDAY*   *BIRTHDAY*   *ANNIVERSARY*

     OTHER: _____

Address of Recipient: _____

Gift From: _____ *Donor Address:* _____

Donor Email: _____

I AM ENCLOSING A CHECK FOR $ $_____ PAYABLE TO HABITAT FOR HUMANITY OR PLEASE CHARGE MY VISA OR MASTERCARD *(CIRCLE ONE)*

Card Number _____ Expiration Date: _____

Name as it appears on Credit Card _____ Charge Amount $ _____

Signature _____

Billing Address _____

Telephone # Day _____ Eve _____

PLEASE NOTE: Your contribution is tax-deductible to the fullest extent allowed by law.
Habitat for Humanity • P.O. Box 1443 • Newport News, VA 23601 • 757-596-5553
www.HelpHabitatforHumanity.org

Printed in the USA
CPSIA information can be obtained
at www.ICGtesting.com
JSHW052016140824
68134JS00027B/2505